This book is part of the Goodyear Series in Education, ...sity of Florida, Editor

...S IN GENERAL METHODS & CENTERS

...Generating and Testing Knowledge
John McCollum

A CALENDAR OF HOME/SCHOOL ACTIVITIES
Jo Anne Patricia Brosnahan and Barbara Walters Milne

CHANGE FOR CHILDREN   Ideas and Activities for Individualizing Learning
Sandra N. Kaplan, Jo Ann B. Kaplan, Sheila K. Madsen, Bette K. Taylor

CREATING A LEARNING ENVIRONMENT   A Learning Center Handbook
Ethel Breyfogle, Susan Nelson, Carol Pitts, Pamela Santich

THE LEARNING CENTER BOOK   An Integrated Approach
Tom Davidson, Phyllis Fountain, Rachel Grogan, Verl Short, Judy Steely,
Katherine Freeman

*ONE AT A TIME ALL AT ONCE   The Creative Teacher's Guide to
Individualized Instruction Without Anarchy*
Jack E. Blackburn and W. Conrad Powell

OPEN SESAME   A Primer in Open Education
Evelyn M. Carswell and Darrell L. Roubinek

*THE OTHER SIDE OF THE REPORT CARD   A How-to-Do-It Program for
Affective Education*
Larry Chase

THE TEACHER'S CHOICE   Ideas and Activities for Teaching Basic Skills
Sandra N. Kaplan, Sheila K. Madsen, Bette T. Gould

*TEACHING FOR LEARNING   Applying Educational Psychology in the
Classroom*
Myron H. Dembo

*OTHER WAYS, OTHER MEANS   Altered Awareness Activities for Receptive
Learning*
Alton Harrison and Diann Musial

*WILL THE REAL TEACHER PLEASE STAND UP?   A Primer in Humanistic
Education, 2nd edition*
Mary Greer and Bonnie Rubinstein

A YOUNG CHILD EXPERIENCES   Activities for Teaching and Learning
Sandra N. Kaplan, Jo Ann B. Kaplan, Sheila K. Madsen, Bette T. Gould

For information about these, or Goodyear books in Language Arts,
Reading, Science, Math, and Social Studies, write to

JANET JACKSON
Goodyear Publishing Company
1640 Fifth Street
Santa Monica, CA 90401
(213) 393-6731

Who's Teaching~

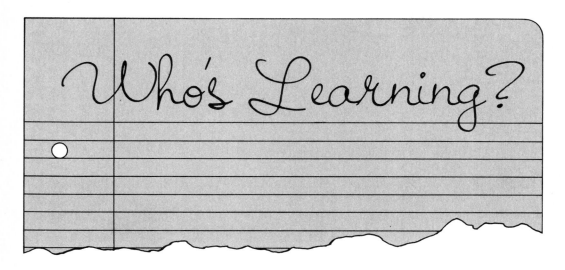

Active Learning in Elementary Schools

DALE L. BRUBAKER

University of North Carolina at Greensboro

Goodyear Publishing Company, Inc.

Santa Monica, California

Library of Congress Cataloging in Publication Data

Brubaker, Dale L
 Who's teaching, who's learning?

 (Goodyear series in education)
 Includes bibliographical references.
 1.   Elementary school teaching—Handbooks, manuals,
etc.   I.   Title
LB1555.B82   372.1'1'02   79—9963
ISBN 0—87620—956—8

Copyright © 1979 by Goodyear Publishing Company, Inc.
Santa Monica, California 90401

Current printing (last digit):
10 9 8 7 6 5 4 3 2 1

ISBN: 0—87620—956—8

Y—9568—0

Printed in the United States of America

For the prospective and inservice
teachers who will work and play
their way through the experiences
in this book, and for the friends
who made this book possible

Contents

Preface xi

Introduction: How to Use This Book 1
    The Approach 2
    Methods and Materials 2
    Ways of Making These Lesson Plans Your Own 3
    Lesson A Transportation 4
    Lesson B Vocations 6
    Evaluating Progress with Lessons 7
    Bon Voyage! 15

PART ONE   Wonderful Me 17

    Chapter 1   Centering Oneself as a Teacher 18
    Thinking, Feeling, and Acting 18
        Self-Inventory 1 19
    Work and Play 24
        Self-Inventory 2 25
        Self-Inventory 3 26
    Conflict and Commitment 31
        Self-Inventory 4 32
        Self-Inventory 5 35

    Chapter 2   Centering and the Creation of Instructional Settings 37
    Integrating Thinking, Feeling, and Acting 38
        Lesson 1   Feeling and Expressing Anger 38
        Lesson 2   What Bugs You? 39
        Lesson 3   Celebrations 41
        Lesson 4   My Own Postage Stamp 42
        Lesson 5   What Is Your Name? 43
        Lesson 6   The Name Game 44
        Lesson 7   Each of Us Is Unique 45
        Lesson 8   Facing Conflict 46
        Lesson 9   Why Me, Teacher? 47
        Lesson 10   Divorce 48

Discovering New Relationships Between Work and Play   **51**
    Lesson 11   Going with the Flow   **52**
    Lesson 12   Immersing Oneself in an Activity   **54**
    Lesson 13   Career Education   **57**
    Lesson 14   Careers and Jobs   **58**
    Lesson 15   Career Symbols   **59**
    Lesson 16   Use of Leisure Time   **60**
Suggested Activities   **62**
Learning About Conflict and Commitment   **62**
    Lesson 17   Commitment and the Acceptance of Responsibility   **62**
    Lesson 18   The Lemonade Stand   **65**
    Lesson 19   What Do You Know About Safety?   **67**
    Lesson 20   Reacting to Safety Hazards   **68**
    Lesson 21   Responsibility of a Citizen   **69**
Conclusion   **70**
Notes   **71**

PART TWO   And You Make Two . . . and More . . .   73

Chapter 3   Where I Stand as a Teacher on Key Issues   74
    Self-Inventory 6   **74**
Attitudes Toward the Community   **79**
    Self-Inventory 7   **79**
Cultural Influences   **85**
    Self-Inventory 8   **85**
Organizational Influences   **88**
    Self-Inventory 9   **89**

**Chapter 4   Creating Settings for Learning About Cultures, Organizations,
    and Communities   93**
The Need for Community   **93**
    Lesson 22   Belonging to a Community   **94**
    Lesson 23   Immigrants   **95**
    Lesson 24   "Ins" and "Outs"   **96**
    Lesson 25   Preferential Treatment   **98**
    Lesson 26   Loyalty to Community   **101**
    Lesson 27   Intolerance   **102**
    Lesson 28   A Fear of Differences   **103**
    Lesson 29   Gaining Acceptance in a New Community   **106**
    Lesson 30   James Goes to School   **108**
    Lesson 31   Conformity   **110**
    Lesson 32   Simple Kindnesses   **111**
    Lesson 33   Adoption   **112**
    Lesson 34   Family Rules, Responsibilities, and Opportunities   **113**
    Lesson 35   Building a Go-Kart   **114**
    Lesson 36   School Rules, Responsibilities, and Opportunities   **116**
    Lesson 37   Political Processes   **118**
    Lesson 38   Landlord-Tenant Confrontation   **119**
Suggested Activities   **121**
    Lesson 39   Relating to Friends   **122**
    Lesson 40   New Friends at Camp   **123**
    Lesson 41   Telling on a Friend   **124**
    Lesson 42   A Retired Friend   **126**
    Lesson 43   Today and Yesterday   **127**
Cultural Influences   **128**
    Lesson 44   What Is A Culture?   **128**
    Lesson 45   Comparing Cultures   **129**

Contents

Lesson 46   Verbal/Nonverbal Communication   **131**
Lesson 47   Communication Problems   **133**
Lesson 48   Nonverbal Communication   **134**
Lesson 49   Communication Networks   **135**
Understanding Organizational Influences   **137**
Suggested Activities   **137**
Lesson 50   Territoriality   **138**
Lesson 51   Attitudes Toward Huge Organizations   **139**
Lesson 52   Assessing Information about Organizations   **140**
Lesson 53   Compromising Withing Organizations   **141**
Lesson 54   How Do You Feel About Compromises?   **142**
Lesson 55   Henry Ford Builds a Car   **144**
Conclusion   **145**
Notes   **146**

PART THREE   . . . on Planet Earth   147

Chapter 5   Environmental Education   148
Self-Inventory 10   **150**

Chapter 6   We're All In It Together   155
Energy Conservation   **156**
Lesson 56   Learning About Energy   **156**
Lesson 57   Conserving Energy in the Home   **157**
Lesson 58   Preparing for Loss of Electricity   **158**
Lesson 59   Save That Tree!   **160**
Suggested Activities   **160**
Fighting Pollution   **161**
Lesson 60   L.J. Builds a Treehouse   **161**
Lesson 61   Looking for Bottles   **164**
Lesson 62   Down with the Litterbug!   **166**
Lesson 63   The Swamp   **168**
Lesson 64   Water Pollution   **169**
Lesson 65   Air Pollution   **170**
Lesson 66   Noise Pollution   **171**
Lesson 67   Treating the Problem of Noise Pollution   **172**
Lesson 68   Silence Is Golden   **174**
Suggested Activities   **175**
Population Control   **176**
Lesson 69   The Population Explosion   **176**
Lesson 70   Density and Crowding   **178**
Lesson 71   Population Changes   **180**
The Child's World   **181**
Lesson 72   Controls for Our Pet Population   **181**
Lesson 73   Caring for a Pet   **182**
Back to Nature   **183**
Lesson 74   Camping Out   **183**
Lesson 75   Preparing to Camp Out   **184**
Lesson 76   A Garden Tour   **185**
Lesson 77   Harvest   **186**
Lesson 78   How Does Your Garden Grow?   **187**
Lesson 79   Organic Gardening   **188**
Lesson 80   Building a Nature Trail   **189**
Lesson 81   Back-to-Nature Careers   **190**
Conclusion   191

Epilogue   191

Preface

The theme and thesis of *Who's Teaching—Who's Learning?* is that the teacher's own growth, development, and learning are basic to the creation of effective learning settings. Books and articles for prospective and inservice teachers sometimes leave us with the impression that schools are only for students. This view appeals to the missionary spirit in each of us, but a moment's reflection raises the question *Who helps the helper?* The answer is that all those within an instructional setting must both *get* and *give* in order to keep a finely honed growing edge.

The three part titles in *Who's Teaching—Who's Learning?* convey the belief that elementary schools should stimulate the participant to better understand himself or herself, others, and the environment. Part One, "Wonderful Me . . . ," presents the optimistic view that each of us has a "wonderful me" that can flower and grow as we better understand ourselves. Part Two, "And You Make Two . . . and More . . . ," makes clear the importance of our relationships with other people, groups, organizations, institutions, and nations. Part Three, "On Planet Earth," was written to help us understand the sensitivity each of us needs in relating to our physical environment. Our Technetronic Age, with its increasing number of gadgets, has indeed been a mixed blessing; we are only now beginning to fathom the dimensions of the relationship between technetronic advances and a fragile environment.

The chapters in *Who's Teaching—Who's Learning?* begin with a dialogue designed to stimulate teachers, whether prospective or inservice, to honestly appraise where they are compared to where they would like to be. Communication between the "I am" and the "I may be" provides the impetus for one's learning, for our vitality is as great as our intentionality.[1] The introductory materials in each chapter are followed by suggested learning experiences, in the form of lesson plans, anecdotes, and other related materials for use with children in instructional settings.

Who's Teaching—Who's Learning? has been written to meet the challenge of translating and applying significant scholarly findings. It is both possible and desirable to translate important findings in educational research into simple and understandable terms. The elementary teacher doesn't have the resources, particularly time and energy, to adopt the lifestyle of a full-time scholar, but can profit from the explorations of the scholar. Some very interesting inquiries and writings have centered on what our society and culture have taught us about the relationship between work and play. These explorations have very important implications for the creation of elementary school instructional settings.

The relationship between ephemeral and persistent issues is also addressed in this book. Some topics are temporarily in vogue. Behind each of these subjects are more persistent, enduring issues that deserve our attention. What is in the news yesterday, today, and tomorrow will vary, but how people learn to resolve or reconcile conflict is a persistent issue common to most news events. *Who's Teaching—Who's Learning?* identifies and addresses persistent rather than fleeting issues.

Making decisions and being part of a nurturing instructional setting can help you form a positive self-concept, a major aim of education and schooling. Invitations to learning, however, communicate a sense of being responsible, able, and valuable.[2] The goal of *Who's Teaching—Who's Learning?* is to issue each of you a positive invitation to learn in the same way that the invitation *Would you like to dance?* communicates the wonderful feeling of being asked to join the dance.

Finally, I wish to issue each of you an invitation I have always wanted to make in my writing. Please drop me a line and tell me what happened to you when you read this book.

Dale L. Brubaker
School of Education
University of North Carolina
at Greensboro
Greensboro, N.C. 27412

Notes

1. Paul Tillich, *The Courage to Be* (New Haven: Yale University Press, 1952), pp. 81–82.
2. William Purkey, *Inviting School Success* (Belmont, Calif.: Wadsworth, 1978).

Who's Teaching— Who's Learning?

Active Learning in Elementary Schools

Introduction: How to Use This Book

Teachers often say that a book provides theories but fails to translate them into practical suggestions for the classroom. On the other hand, those who are more interested in theory criticize "how to do it" books for not having any kind of theoretical framework. The challenge is clear: *How can a book have practical value in elementary schools and still communicate its theory in a way that makes sense?*

Who's Teaching—Who's Learning? was written to meet this challenge. It contains many practical suggestions of value to the prospective and inservice teacher and yet these suggestions are part of a conceptual framework which consists of: (1) a carefully stated rationale for the overall approach used in the book as well as a rationale (objectives) for the use of each lesson; (2) a variety of methods and materials consistent with the rationale of the book; and (3) suggestions for evaluating both teacher and student progress.

The learning experiences suggested by the author are designed to encourage teachers to add their own objectives, methods and materials, and evaluation procedures. In other words, the planned curriculum and the spontaneous curriculum are accounted for by recognizing the importance of what evolves from particular lessons. The teacher should be the artist who orchestrates such spontaneous interactions.

The Approach

Who's Teaching—Who's Learning? tries to actively motivate teachers and
students in several ways. First, teachers and students are asked to identify and give reasons for their own values and the values of others that
support or conflict. Second, the learner is encouraged to role play positive and negative relations between individuals and between groups on a
given topic. That is, there are very real differences among people as they
argue for their points of view, and such diversity is useful in stimulating
dialogue and inquiry—painful though this process is at times. Role playing invites the learner to try on different roles in a relatively low-risk
setting. Third, the teacher and student in a learning setting are expected
to reconstruct their own values in light of analysis or else defend their
values. In short, value identification, value clarification, and value construction are the heart of the materials in this book. The reader is urged
to be a participant rather than a spectator.

In *Who's Teaching—Who's Learning?* I call attention to pressing
matters facing mankind in general and our society in particular. Urbani-
zation, suburbanization, ruralization, technological change, ecology,
safety, communication, intergroup relations, and intragroup relations
serve as examples. Although some of these topics are relatively new addi-
tions to our daily language, other topics have been and will continue to
be persistent issues to be faced by us, by our children, and by our children's children. There is little chance that the themes presented will be
quickly dated.

Methods and Materials

The materials in *Who's Teaching—Who's Learning?* can serve as a
springboard for action projects in the total school and community. Many
of the experiences in the lesson plans invite the teacher and students to
involve people outside the classroom. For example, other teachers and
students in the school, the principal, and parents can be important participants in the learning process if suggestions in the lesson plans are
implemented. Students and the teacher are also urged to relate to
people and groups outside the school by making contact with them in
their places of work and play. This book is consistent with major ideas

from the community education movement that has had such an impact on education in this country in recent years.

When involved in lessons in the book, students and teachers can structure their learning around key organizing concepts, such as multiple causation, culture, ecology, communication, and occupations. If learned in one setting, these concepts can be useful to the student in a different setting. This way of organizing learning is in marked contrast to the memorization of many different and often unrelated bits of information for further recall. In essence, the child can construct a conceptual framework that will be invaluable in the decision-making process throughout life. Concepts in this framework draw from a number of disciplines such as science, language arts, social studies, and reading. This integration of learnings from the various disciplines helps the teacher focus on the child as learner rather than on a particular discipline.

Who's Teaching—Who's Learning? includes the teacher in the learning process by defining his or her role as that of coordinator, catalyst, and fellow clarifier, which is quite different from the traditional role of authoritarian moral judge and dispenser of knowledge. This view of teacher education is consistent with the thesis that the teacher must receive at a high level in order to give at a high level.[1]

Experiences in *Who's Teaching—Who's Learning?* provide the teacher with another approach to elementary school teaching. It simply makes good sense that the teacher shouldn't use a single approach but should draw from a reservoir of approaches to teaching. In most cases, the materials in this book will serve as a complement to what the teacher is already doing.

Ways of Making These Lesson Plans Your Own

Each of us has the urge to make what we learn our own by revising it in some way. The enthusiasm that accompanies this creative process serves as the vitality for our own instruction and learning as teachers. The lesson plans in *Who's Teaching—Who's Learning?* have served to stimulate hundreds of teachers to create their own variations on the materials. This pilot program has taken place throughout the United States.[2] The sample lessons in this section illustrate how teachers planned their use of the materials and how they felt when they actually used a particular lesson.

The following lesson on transportation serves as an example.

LESSON A   TRANSPORTATION

Objectives: As a result of this lesson, students will be able to:
(1) identify four means of transportation;
(2) recognize pictures of different modes of transportation and suggest where one would go to use each type;
(3) give reasons why we need transportation; and
(4) express a personal desire to use various kinds of transportation.

Methods and Materials:
1. Read the following story to the class:

   One time I decided to take a trip to visit a friend in a city a long way from here. I knew it was too far to walk and so I had to figure out a way to get there. I got into my car (hold up a picture of a car) and drove to the train station (show picture of a train). The train took me to a city where I got a taxi to the airport. I got into a plane (hold up a picture of an airplane). After flying to another city's airport I got on a bus (hold up a picture of a bus) with a lot of other people. The bus took me to a street corner and I walked to my friend's house.

2. The following questions will aid the discussion:
   a. Which means of travel (transportation) did I drive myself? (See if students can define ways of travel as transportation rather than giving away the word "transportation.")
   b. Which kind of transportation was in the air most of the time? On the land?
   c. Which kind of transportation was the fastest? The slowest?
   d. What kinds of transportation have you used? How did it feel to travel this way?
   e. Take a school bus to the airport, then have students list the main questions they would like to ask airport officials.
   f. Ask the students if anything in our country has changed because of the automobile.

3. Have each child draw a picture of his favorite way of traveling. Post pictures around the classroom along with pictures children get from magazines, travel offices, etc.

Evaluation: Observe reactions of students to the story and their behavior throughout the lesson. Bring in a picture of an ocean liner and have them raise questions about this means of travel.

Let us now turn to a teacher's description of how she planned for instruction in a third grade class, and how she reacted to the actual implementation of her plan:

I began by reading the original lesson plan. It seemed to be pretty simple and so I began collecting pictures of different kinds of transportation. Later I read the lesson plan again and it didn't seem so easy because I wanted to bring some things into the lesson that would be different. I wanted to add something at the beginning to catch the interest of the children. One idea I considered was to have a record with a lot of different kinds of transportation sounds, but the media center and city library didn't have anything to fit my needs. I then asked a couple of other teachers for suggestions and somebody suggested a regular old rubber tire wheel. This raised more questions: How do we use the wheel in transportation and how important is the wheel to various kinds of transportation?

Now it seemed appropriate to return to some of the questions asked in the original lesson plan. I particularly liked the question "What kinds of transportation have you children used?" and so I decided to begin with this question. For a follow-up activity I added a group game for the children to do. The children would be divided into groups of threes and given a transportation problem. For example, "If you were in Chicago and needed to get to Los Angeles in the next twelve hours, what kinds of transportation could you use?" I also decided to use a globe or map to show the children how far the people in the problem had to go.

The children responded quite well to the lesson and came up with a lot of answers I hadn't thought of myself. They really seemed to like the pictures of the different kinds of transportation. One boy, however, tried to look at the picture order ahead of time and tell everybody the answer ahead of time. Children were very eager to answer the questions and they were most interested in what kinds of transportation I had used in my life. When I passed out the cards with the transportation problems and asked them if they needed any help, they said that they could do it by themselves. The children really seemed to understand the concept of transportation and travel and in the process used comparisons and contrasts between different kinds of transportation.

The following lesson plan was used by a teacher of young children.

LESSON B   VOCATIONS

Objectives: As a result of this lesson, students will be able to explain how the following factors can influence a person's choice of a vocation:

(1) whether the work is inside or outside;

(2) the amount of money the job pays;

(3) the amount and kind of education required; and

(4) the opinion of others (family, friends) about how desirable the job is (the status of the occupation).

Methods and Materials:

1. Say to the class, "Your fathers and mothers, your uncles and aunts, brothers and sisters may have jobs. Can you name some of these jobs or kinds of work?"

2. Write students' suggestions on the blackboard. If a range of occupations is not voluntarily given, stimulate suggestions with suggestions of your own.

3. Choose four jobs from the list you have written on the board and place each at the top of a column on the board, as follows:
   nurse   doctor   mailperson   switchboard operator

4. Discuss why people choose such jobs. In filling the columns, feature the four variables in the Objectives and any others that arise (such as "Are both men and women encouraged to take this job and have things been changing recently in this regard?")

nurse	*doctor*	*mailperson*	*switchboard operator*
usually works inside	inside	outside-inside	inside
average salary	high salary	average salary	low to average
a few years after high school	a lot of years after high school	learn on job after high school	learn on job
used to be only for women but now also for men	most think this is a good job, more women now becoming doctors.	more women now doing this	few men do this

Evaluation: List jobs of people in the school. Discuss each in terms of how variables apply.

The teacher described her encounter with the lesson plan in the following manner:

> I added to the original lesson plan on vocations by bringing in paper bags and having the children create puppets by drawing pictures of people performing different jobs. Each child explained what the person did using the puppet to do the talking. They really got into the lesson in this way. Then I asked them what parents and other adults they knew did. I began this discussion by wearing my father's fire hat.
>
> Then I divided the class into smaller groups of three and four children and gave them a card with a career on it to pantomime for the rest of the class. Each group had to decide what it wished to pantomime. Two boys acted out how a paramedic would help a person in distress. One boy was stretched out on the floor and the other was the paramedic. (They got the idea from a television show.) One girl was a doctor who worked in a clinic. (She got this idea from a soap opera on television.) One boy was a football star who ran around the room climbing over tacklers. The groups that weren't doing the pantomime at the time guessed what the pantomimers were doing. This worked out well as they love to guess rather than being told.
>
> At the end of the lesson I pointed out that jobs are becoming more and more open to women and they (the students) can try to have any career they want regardless of age, sex, race, and so on. (I wondered if I sermonized too much on this and I think I'll return later to this topic and get more student discussion.)
>
> What the children enjoyed most was the active participation and I learned a good deal about their career ideas.

Evaluating Progress with Lessons

Prospective and inservice teachers are aware of some of the things that happen when they use the lesson plans described in this book: prospective teachers usually involve themselves in peer teaching or videotaped teaching situations, whereas inservice teachers usually rely on their memories of what happened when the lesson was taught. Even so, being involved in the teaching act makes it difficult to evaluate many of the more subtle interactions in the instructional setting. For this reason we have urged those who use the plans to get colleagues' responses to their teaching and also use any mechanical means possible for feedback and evaluation. The following suggestions for evaluating teacher progress are based on what we have learned from these evaluation procedures.

Our suggestions are in the form of "pitfalls" facing the teacher, but such "pitfalls" should also be viewed as opportunities for improving instruction.

Pitfall 1: The teacher calls on the same students repeatedly, thus failing to give all students the opportunity to articulate their ideas and feelings. A teacher became aware of the fact that she talked more to students closest to the front of the classroom. She therefore moved around the room more while deliberately trying to bring out responses from students who were less active in class conversations. She also recognized her bias for those students who quickly raised their hands in response to her questions. Consequently she began calling on students who didn't raise their hands in order to involve them in class dialogue. She reminded herself in the process to give students time to answer questions rather than quickly moving on to students who immediately had the answer.

Pitfall 2: The teacher consistently plays the role of actor (initiator) and the students play the role of reactor. Students and the teacher share three sources of power: expertise, charisma, and support. Expertise appears in forms such as reading, writing, and speaking. Although most students have less expertise in reading, writing, and speaking than the teacher, they nevertheless can tap this source of power to get some of the things they want in the instructional setting. Charisma, that intangible ability to motivate others, is also a source of power for both the teacher and students. The ability to coach and counsel others is the source of power known as support: "I know you can do it" is the message that brings out the best in each of us.

The one source of power the teacher has but the students don't have is positional authority. By virtue of his or her position of authority in the school, the teacher traditionally stands up more in the classroom, occupies space in the front of the room more, and generally sets the stage for student activities. Traditional expectations of the role of teacher plus positional authority to continue to enforce such expectations can lead to an instructional setting in which the teacher consistently initiates and acts, with students consistently reacting. (There is a certain irony in the school's rhetoric that upon leaving school the student will be the kind of good citizen who is comfortable in acting as well as reacting. This is coupled with the school's contention that it is preparing the student for such a responsibility although in fact the student is better prepared to be a reactor than an actor.)

The effective teacher learns that there are times when students and the teacher can cooperatively create instructional settings in which all feel free to initiate when they feel this is appropriate. The teacher learns to suspend positional authority so that communication can be horizontal as well as vertical. When communication is repeatedly vertical, the student is being indoctrinated to accept bureaucratic decision-making patterns: those higher up in the organization always give commands down (vertically) to those who are lower in the organization.

Pitfall 3: The teacher not only consistently initiates but also serves as a filter for conversation between students. In other words, students talk through the teacher without talking to each other. All of us have experienced this in traditional classroom settings with students seated in rows and the teacher standing behind a lectern. The higher the grade level the more we tend to see this kind of instructional setting. The payoff for the teacher is the security of controlling communication and therefore seeming to control the students. But in effect those students who want to use power exercise it over the teacher but not the students. That is, the game is to persuade the teacher rather than other students. Since the teacher dispenses grades, the currency of the school, he or she can use this currency as a means of reinforcing a position of authority. The teacher who consistently filters classroom dialogue creates a formal learning setting at the expense of informal learning.

Pitfall 4: The teacher consistently asks questions that can only lead to simple "correct" answers. This is the most common pitfall faced by prospective teachers. Listen to the following dialogue in which the teacher not only expects the "right" answer but often gives it to the students because of anxiety.

TEACHER: Communication is a word that means how we tell other people how we feel about something. When I open my mouth to tell you something, what do I use to communicate with you?

STUDENT: Your mouth.

TEACHER: No! What comes out of my mouth?

STUDENT: Words.

TEACHER: That's right. And when I look at you, what do I use to communicate?

STUDENT: Your eyes.

TEACHER: Good.

The teacher didn't discuss the characteristics of communication so that the students would then discover and articulate the concept "communication"; rather, she immediately defined the concept for the students and then guided them to simple "correct" answers.

In order to better understand different levels of questioning, let us study a seven-level model that begins with low-level questions and progresses to higher levels.[3] The model is in the form of a tally sheet so that the teacher can record the number of questions asked at a particular level as well as the percentage of total questions asked at that level.

Classroom Question Tally Sheet

Category	Description	Number of Questions	% of Total Questions Asked
1. Memory	Student recalls or recognizes information.		
2. Translation	Student changes information into a different symbolic form or language.		
3. Interpretation	Student discovers relationships among facts, generalizations, definitions, values, and skills.		
4. Application	Student solves a lifelike problem that requires the identification of the issue and the selection and use of appropriate generalizations and skills.		
5. Analysis	Student solves a problem in the light of conscious knowledge of the parts and forms of thinking.		
6. Synthesis	Student solves a problem that requires original, creative thinking.		
7. Evaluation	Student makes a judgment of good or bad, right or wrong, according to standards designated by students.		

Memory questions are asked in order to have the student recall information supposedly learned. Examples of such questions are: "Who is the president of the United States?" "What is the capital of North Carolina?" Although one of the "lowest" forms of questions with respect to stimulation of thinking, memory questions have played a significant role in elementary school teaching. The textbook has traditionally been the fact center for memory questions. The key issues with respect to memory questions center on what is worth remembering and how questions can be structured most efficiently in order to emphasize what is worth remembering. There are two main problems with memorizing information other than the fact that it doesn't stimulate high level thinking: (1) much information is quickly dated, and (2) the student quickly forgets information previously memorized. An example of outdated information comes immediately to mind: having memorized that there are forty-eight states in the United States, the author must now remind himself to add Alaska and Hawaii. With respect to the second problem, research indicates that information memorized is quickly forgotten.[4]

To *translate* is to transfer original meaning into one's own words. Synonyms serve as an example. Questions are often phrased in such a way that the student is asked to read the text and then tell what it means. Students are sometimes asked to translate their ideas into a drawing or poetry or to translate the meaning of a picture or poem into their own words.

To *interpret* is to make sense out of particular ideas by establishing relationships between them. Some of the different kinds of relationships established by answering interpretative questions are: comparative, implicative, the forming of inductive generalizations based on supporting evidence, quantitative, and cause and effect.[5] Examples of these relationships are:

Comparative. What differences and similarities are there between houses in the United States and England?

Implicative. If an Eskimo moves from his igloo into a house in a town, what do you think would happen to change his way of life (culture)?

Inductive Generalizations. Now that we've studied black culture, what needs can we say that this culture meets?

Quantitative. How many people live in our city?

Cause and Effect. What usually happens in your home when there is a power outage?

The main aim of the teacher who uses *application* questions is to present problems that the student will actually face in life outside of school. If children learn to think of safety in crossing the street as part of their instruction in school, they are expected to use this understanding in situations outside the school setting.

Analysis questions require the student to take apart the elements of a system and understand the relationships among these parts. For example, the teacher may ask, "What are the three levels of government in the United States and how do they relate to each other?" Or, "What materials are used in building a dog house and how are they used in order to build the house?"

Synthesis questions challenge children to integrate their ideas into new and imaginative forms. For example, children in one school were asked to suggest ideas for redecorating their classroom so that it had a new look.

Questions designed to elicit *evaluative statements* from children require them to build a value system and see how closely an idea or product fits into this system. Students in one classroom were asked to evaluate the Star Spangled Banner as a national anthem. In another setting, children were asked whether or not staying in during recess was an acceptable or fair punishment for misbehavior in the classroom.

The various levels of questions are helpful in that they make the teacher conscious of the kind of thinking and feeling elicited by a particular question. Since our questions tend to fall into patterns, the tally sheet can be useful in bringing such patterns into our consciousness, after which we can try out different ways of questioning.

Pitfall 5: The teacher simply doesn't give students enough time to think before answering questions. In our discussion of the previous pitfall we saw that low-level questions are easy to answer quickly for they presuppose a "right" answer that one can memorize for easy recognition. Higher level questions are a different matter, however, for they involve more sophisticated cognitive processes. Such questions take time to think through. M. B. Rowe has identified the time the teacher allows for a student's response as wait-time.[6] Her research indicates that the average wait-time of teachers is approximately one second. After reviewing Rowe's research, William Purkey suggests

> that when teachers increase their wait-time from the usual one second to three to five seconds, the length of student responses increases, the number of unsolicited but appropriate responses increases, and failure to respond decreases.[7]

We can therefore see that the qualitative nature of the question, such as its open-endedness, and the amount of wait-time allowed by the teacher are significant dimensions of interaction within instructional settings.

Pitfall 6: Students aren't encouraged to become involved in the valu-

ing process because the teacher has already determined "correct" values for the students and has structured the instructional setting accordingly. Each of us naturally has a value system but teachers vary as to (1) the extent to which they feel values should be questioned and (2) their commitment to the creation of instructional settings where such questioning can take place. The following dialogue demonstrates the importance of a sense of playfulness in this questioning process:

> STUDENT: Sometimes when we communicate we twitch our nose in a funny way. I always look at people's noses when they talk.
> TEACHER: I hadn't thought of that but it makes sense. I wonder if there are some other ways we communicate that we haven't talked about yet.

In this example the teacher's value system wasn't challenged. Imagine for a moment a teacher who is highly structured *all the time.* The following dialogue took place at the Natural Science Center on a field trip:

> TEACHER: Stay in line as you move by the exhibits so that we have a nice orderly group.
> STUDENT: Some of us are more interested in some exhibits than in others. Can we look at those longer as the rest of the group goes by?
> TEACHER: No! Just move along with the line!

The student challenged order and control, basic elements of the teacher's value system. There was no follow-up discussion of the need for a high degree of order and control in some situations but not in others. The child was simply told "Obey!" When children are encouraged to become involved in value identification, clarification, and reconstruction, they accomplish more than a better understanding of their own and others' values. They also participate in settings in which they improve basic communication skills: they voice their views to others and develop political potency by trying to persuade others. They learn to face conflict rather than to run from it, which in turn gives them the opportunity to express both positive and negative feelings in a public forum. The result is a more positive self-concept.

Another teacher strongly values a more open instructional setting where students seldom form lines or meet together as a whole class with all students doing the same assignment. She prides herself on her interest centers and individualized instruction packets whereby each student signs a contract for the work he or she hopes to complete within a certain period of time. The following dialogue occurred during the first week of class in the fall:

> TEACHER: Children, we'll now move to our interest centers. George, you go to the center where they're working on math facts.
>
> STUDENT: I'm not used to working on math that way. (The child had earlier in the week brought a letter from home in which his mother criticized the lack of structure in the classroom because she didn't think her son would learn his basics.)
>
> TEACHER: Just move to your centers everybody!

There was no follow-up discussion in which reasons for and against particular structures for learning were aired. The teacher's commitment to the open classroom was so strong that those who opposed or even questioned this commitment were considered "wrong."

The two examples just cited demonstrate that the extent or degree to which the teacher questions his or her own values and the way in which he or she helps create instructional settings with respect to values education are more important than the fact that some value systems are labeled conservative and others are labeled liberal.

Pitfall 7: The teacher experiences goal displacement. We observe goal displacement in all facets of our lives. For example, the parents of two children, ages eight and ten, originally wanted to spend the evening at a good restaurant with the whole family. The two children fought so much in the back seat of the car that the parents turned around, took the children home, and placed them in the care of a babysitter. At this point the parents were at a forked road situation: (1) they could have let this incident ruin their evening even though the children were now safely in the care of a babysitter, or (2) they could proceed to have a good time at the restaurant themselves. If they had taken the former course they would have been victims of goal displacement: their original goal, to have a good time, would have been displaced by the goal of letting the incident bother them for the remainder of the evening. This same kind of process works in elementary school instructional settings. The teacher has chosen several important goals to pursue, but one student's misbehavior becomes the focus of the lesson for all of the students. The challenge to the teacher is to relate to the child's misbehavior as efficiently and effectively as possible without letting this incident take over the lesson. The difficulty of this challenge shouldn't be underestimated, for some incidents play on the teacher's emotions more than others.

Bon Voyage!

It is hoped that you will have an exciting journey through the pages of this book. The lesson plans and experiences you encounter are designed to be both fun and challenging. In the beginning of each of the following parts, you will be involved in a series of activities and discussions designed to stimulate an honest appraisal of your present positions with respect to issues discussed in the chapter; then, a number of learning experiences and activities are included, in lesson plan form, so that students and other participants in schools can be involved with teachers giving leadership to the creation of settings that focus on the issues discussed in the beginning of the part.

As you participate in this venture, please send any reactions and suggestions to me at the address on page xii and I promise a reply.

NOTES

1. Seymour B. Sarason, *The Culture of the School and the Problem of Change* (Boston: Allyn and Bacon, 1971), p. 167.

2. Materials were developed as part of the University of North Carolina at Greensboro Humanistic Education Project.

3. Gary Manson and Ambrose A. Clegg, Jr., "Classroom Questions: Keys to Children's Thinking?" *Peabody Journal of Education*, 47, no. 5 (1970), pp. 304–5. The best original source on questioning is Norris M. Sanders, *Classroom Questions* (New York: Harper and Row, 1966).

4. See John DeCecco and Arlene Richards, *Growing Pains: Uses of School Conflict* (New York: Aberdeen, 1974), p. 36.

5. Sanders, *op. cit.*, pp. 44–60.

6. M. B. Rowe, "Wait-time and Rewards as Instructional Variables, Their Influence on Language, Logic and Fate-control: Part I," *Journal of Research in Science Teaching*, 2, no. 2 (1974), pp. 81–94; and M. B. Rowe, "Relation of Wait-time and Rewards to the Development of Language, Logic and Fate-control: Part II," *Journal of Research in Science Teaching*, 2, no. 4 (1974), pp. 290–308.

7. William Purkey, *Inviting School Success* (Belmont, Calif.: Wadsworth, 1978), p. 73.

PART ONE

Wonderful Me...

It is quite remarkable to hear students describe their characteristics when feeling good about themselves: "I had energy to burn." "My body was erect and I walked with a bounce in my step." "I had a smile that wouldn't quit!" All of these comments point to the fact that when feeling good the person had a "wonderful me" attitude that was reflected in his thinking, feeling, and physical being. Unfortunately, we often learn to collect negative baggage that leads us to the conclusion that we are less than adequate. When this happens to the teacher, it is evident in his or her bearing and both teacher and students suffer. Let us reflect for a few moments on how this state of affairs comes to be and how we can realistically work and play our way out of it.

Chapter 1

Centering Oneself as a Teacher

When asked "Who is the most important person in your life?" teachers usually answer "Myself!" Of course we recognize that one's conception of oneself is formed by relating to others and the environment, but we are still left with the realization that self-understanding is an essential element in being an effective teacher. This chapter is therefore aimed at helping us understand better what it means to be a "centered person."[1] In the process we will consider the various influences that we have allowed to push us off center, with special attention given to the role of formal education. We begin with what we have learned about the relationship of thinking, feeling, and acting.

Thinking, Feeling, and Acting

Our culture, society, and influential organizations have taught us a great deal about how we should relate to our thinking, feeling, and acting. Let us begin to examine these influences with a self-inventory.

SELF-INVENTORY 1

1. Think for a moment of the happiest experience you've had in the last year or two. Briefly describe this experience below:

   _____

   _____

   _____

   _____

   a. When this experience occurred, did you relate to it primarily with your: (Please check one or more.)

      _____ thinking?

      _____ feelings?

      _____ physical movement?

   b. In what ways, if any, did your *formal* education (schooling) prepare you for relating to this experience?

   _____

   _____

   _____

2. Think for a moment of the most difficult and agonizing experience you've had in the last year or two. Briefly describe this experience below:

   _____

   _____

   _____

   _____

    a. When this experience occurred, did you relate to it primarily with your: (Please check one or more.)

        _____ thinking?

        _____ feelings?

        _____ physical movement?

    b. In what ways, if any, did your *formal* education (schooling) prepare you for relating to this experience?

_____

_____

_____

Teachers have answered the first item in the self-inventory with a variety of responses such as: "I got a new job!" "I had a baby!" "I found out I was named teacher of the year!" How did they relate to this good news? They literally jumped with joy for they couldn't contain themselves. In the process they released tremendous feelings of happiness. How did their formal education, particularly in universities, prepare them for relating to their newfound happiness? Little, if at all. As one student remarked, "Our classes were designed to test our ability to memorize and recall information such as the causes of the American Revolution." The kind of cognitive thinking required was of a relatively simple nature. Another student added, "The teacher or professor was free to move about the room and express his feelings but students didn't have this right!" How did students feel about this inequity? "I learned not to question it," said one student. "There were times when I really wanted to express my feelings and actions, but the classroom wasn't set up for that!"

    What kinds of experiences caused students to agonize? Divorce, loss of a loved one such as a parent or grandparent, and difficulties with a friend were often cited. How did this affect the student? "It hit me right in the 'gut' and I had to pace the room," said one student. Others concurred! There was general agreement that their formal education or schooling simply didn't prepare them for such agony and furthermore formal education did little to alleviate their pain at the moment. One student added, "We were too busy covering the material to relate our personal agendas!"

Where did students get help in order to cope with their difficult experiences and where did they go in order to express their personal victories? Peers, parents, and brothers and sisters were most often mentioned and all students agreed that they turned to informal settings in order to vent their feelings and express their actions.

Lest we become too depressed with the fact that much of our formal schooling, particularly in the higher grades and in colleges and universities, has ill prepared us for relating to our emotions, let us turn to how we might find our way out of this puzzle. At the outset it would be well to state a thesis for further examination: centering ourselves, or discovering and maintaining the "wonderful me" that is essential to effective teaching, depends on (1) being honest with oneself about one's feelings in a particular situation, and (2) finding the best way to express such feelings.

The first part of this thesis suggests the importance of being sensitive to one's past as it comes to play in influencing one's present. One teacher commented, "I had to learn that my first inclination in disciplining a student was to treat him just as my father treated me." This awareness demonstrated the teacher's sensitivity to the past. Another teacher said, "My parents taught me that it is okay to express positive feelings such as 'I love you' but it isn't okay to express negative feelings such as 'I hate you'." Knowing this about himself, the teacher could then decide what to do about such knowledge.

Finding what one considers to be the best ways to express honest emotions leads us into the creation of instructional settings in which one can express emotions without fear of failure or reprisal. The teacher can help create settings that provide emotional support for all who are part of them, including the teacher.

You should be honest with yourself about your feelings and find the best way(s) to express such feelings serves as a guideline for the teacher, but what are some practical suggestions for applying the guideline from day to day? The following advice is shared by inservice teachers who participated in an elementary school seminar.

Whenever possible have two or more people from your school visit other schools, attend conferences, and participate in inservice courses. "I used to go alone when I left the school for inservice experiences," commented one teacher, "but when I got back to my school few people understood what I had experienced because they hadn't been there." She added, "I soon went back to my old ways of teaching even though I didn't really want to." This teacher then, had an experience that had an important influence on her inservice education: "I took a really good university course on elementary schools, and Jane—who teaches with me—also took the course." She continued, "When we got back to our school we talked for hours about how we would try out the new ideas in our classrooms. When we tried them out we supported each other when things went wrong and celebrated together when they went right." The two teachers had created an emotional support system which gave them enough security to keep a growing edge in their teaching. The two teachers could be honest with each other as to their feelings about what they had experienced and they had a supportive partner to whom anything and everything could be said.

Have someone in the school who will listen and be discreet about what you say. It is helpful for a teacher to express feelings to a spouse or friend, but this person doesn't really understand the school situation since he or she hasn't directly experienced it. Even a psychiatrist or psychologist is at a disadvantage in not being acquainted with organizational realities faced by the elementary school educator. But another teacher in the school knows the people there and has a feel for the organizational realities. The risk you run, however, in revealing your true feelings to a colleague is the possibility that your friend will be indiscreet, which could lead to difficulties in the school. How does one deal with this reality? "My friend and I have openly talked to each other about the need for honest sharing and the importance of discretion," said one teacher, "and the advantages of such a relationship outweigh the possibility of indiscretion." A friendship can serve as a safety valve for the teacher, for any person in an organization naturally faces problems and dilemmas that tax one's emotional resources. Prospective teachers in teacher education programs also need relationships that allow them to release their feelings: the stakes are high, for one either graduates and gets a teaching credential or one does not.

Recognize that some settings and situations are "sick" and your stress in reacting to such settings is natural. Most of us were taught to be "supermen" and "superwomen" who can handle all situations if we just have the will to do so. The pressure that this myth places on each of us is incredible. In order to deal with this pressure we often repress, which is to say that we don't admit our own feelings to ourselves, let alone find effective ways to express them. The fact is that teachers are people who experience both personal and career passages and the process of experiencing these passages is often very difficult indeed.[2]

To recognize that one is not superman or superwoman is to recognize that some settings and situations are less than healthy and a natural response is to seek outside help. Friends are helpful much of the time, but there are times when each of us can profit from counseling of a more expert nature. Although our society is more open in this respect than previously, there is still some pressure not to admit that we have difficulties that can be lessened with psychological help. And yet those teachers who have sought such help in trying situations usually tell others that they were not only helped but in the process also lost the fear of seeking such help.

Maintain a variety of professional contacts outside your school. Some teachers maintain contact with college friends who also chose teaching as a career. "There were twelve of us who were determined to stay in touch," according to one teacher, "and so we formed a group called the 'Dippy Dozen'." Those who are able get together each New Year's Day for dinner at someone's home. And between times they correspond and meet at conventions and conferences.

The "Dippy Dozen" is actually an informal professional network[3] based on a good deal of trust and caring which in turn invites members to share their feelings about being a teacher. Each of us has the opportunity to build professional networks although it is often difficult to take the first step in consciously doing so. Some teachers occasionally drop by university offices to ask professors about their most recent ideas and in the process get many free materials for use in classrooms. (The professor's ego is also naturally flattered by the questions!) By making contact with professors, teachers also get to know which professors care to be part of their professional networks. Some teachers also write professors, consultants, publishers, and others for information and in the process make professional friends.

The key to building an effective professional network is to take the initiative or play the actor rather than reactor role. One of the most satisfying results of being part of a professional network is to find that other professionals share many of the same problems and dilemmas. A network is a good place to share many of your feelings in an informal way.

Maintain a variety of nonprofessional contacts outside your school. A teacher doesn't have to talk about school matters in order to release feelings. Teachers indicate that it is very satisfying to have friends and acquaintances outside their schools. The feeling transmitted to the teacher from those outside the school in such settings is simply "We like you as a person and enjoy spending time with you!" (What an important message this is in building one's "wonderful me"!) The teacher with contacts outside the school also acquires the confidence that he or she can relate well to others in different settings. Conversely, the teacher who isolates himself or herself in the elementary school acquires the fear that he or she might not be able to function effectively in outside settings. "I want to keep in touch with high school students," said one elementary school teacher, "and so a friend and I team teach a group of ten to twelve high school students each Sunday morning at church." She added, "It's like having another home, for our class is informal and relaxed and it also gives me an excuse to talk to my friend who is in the business world." A second teacher responded: "I've recently been interested in giving speeches because I want to share some of my experiences in traveling overseas. I joined the Toastmaster's Club and we have a lot of fun every Wednesday night." Some teachers join clubs and organizations that combine social fun and physical exercise: "Some of us couples started a racquetball club and the fun we have together a couple of times a week makes the winter tolerable." A change of pace and place can be a kind of self-renewal for the teacher.

Work and play together to create instructional settings in your school that encourage you as well as the children to honestly encounter and express your feelings and actions. Teachers are pleasantly surprised when they cooperatively build instructional settings that encourage everyone to express their feelings more freely. "I really changed the sociology of the classroom," expressed one teacher after using role playing with her children. "I didn't realize how much I could learn about myself and others by having a good team-teaching experience," related another teacher. The traditional classroom setting often left the teacher with the impression that he or she had to be a superman or superwoman solely responsible for the children's learning. The present book is based on the premise that cooperative setting-building and cooperative learning can lead to both teacher and student renewal.

Work and Play

The teacher who learns to integrate feeling, thinking, and acting experiences a kind of balance that is a major part of being centered. A second characteristic of being centered relates to work and play. What has each of us been taught with respect to work and play? Are we conscious of the effect our education in this regard has on what we do, not just in professional areas of concern, but in nonprofessional areas that influence professional areas? What alternative ways of viewing relationships between work and play will cause us to act differently?

Let us begin with a self-inventory:

SELF-INVENTORY 2

How do you react to the following story about a teacher headed for school early in the morning? Can you identify with this teacher in any way? What does this story say about what our culture and society teach concerning the relationship between work and play?

> I got in the car and started for school. Sometimes it seems like the longest ride in the world. I felt my heart beat faster as I got about halfway there. Then as I got closer to the school my heart actually began to flutter. I thought for a moment of being on an island with white sand and blue water and a cool drink in my hand. I pulled up to a traffic light, heard a roar, and looked to my left. A young guy on a motorcycle! Just like that television show where the young guy with the chopper rides off into the blue and the old guy in the car heads off to work. Me with my dress clothes and the young dude on the chopper with casual clothes. He with his freedom of space and time and me closed into my air-conditioned car headed for an air-conditioned new school with walls all around it and a playground with a fence around it. Wish I could just take off like that.
>
> Even my vacations are confining! Kids fighting in the back seat of the car all the way to the campground with people all over each other. I can't even smell the out-of-doors in this air-conditioned car. It's weird. The older I get the less I'm in touch with the simple things that give me more pleasure than living in my cocoon of gadgets and other complexities. I talked to a man who sells recreation vehicles and he said that people come in and want to sell a small camper because they don't like camping, so he talks them into buying a bigger recreational vehicle with lots of gadgets like they have in their homes.
>
> Now I'm almost at the school. Now I'm out of my car and headed toward the doors of the buildings. Sometimes I think they should be revolving doors so that I can just go around and around all day. Well, I'm inside now and headed for my classroom to teach.

In discussing this story, inservice teachers quickly become conscious of many aspects of their professional lives that they have taken for granted. It is much like our simply accepting the fact that a classroom has to have four ninety-degree-angle corners. Ninety-degree-angle corners are a cultural imperative, a subtle "command" that we just accept as an architectural given. Rituals and traditions become habits that aren't questioned because we aren't conscious or aware of other ways of viewing things.

The following self-inventory will help us become more conscious of cultural imperatives with regard to work-play relationships:

SELF-INVENTORY 3

Questions are of a short-answer and open-ended variety. They ask you to make choices, but you are also encouraged to add any other ideas you wish.

1. When the word "work" is brought to your attention, what are some of the things that immediately come to mind?

   _____

   _____

   _____

2. Look at your answers to the previous question. Where do you think you learned to associate these characteristics with work?

   _____

   _____

3. How were you taught to associate these characteristics with work?

   _____

   _____

   _____

4. When the word "play" is brought to your attention, what are some of the things that immediately come to mind?

_____

_____

_____

5. Look at your answers to the previous question. Where do you think you learned to associate these characteristics with play?

_____

_____

_____

6. How were you taught to associate these characteristics with play?

_____

_____

_____

7. _____ _____ Would you say that you tend to make a distinction
      yes   no   between work activities and play activities?

8. Please check one or both of the following blanks if the characteristic usually applies to work and play *in your life*. (In the event that the characteristic doesn't apply, check no blank.)

Work   Play

_____ _____ Suspend gratification or enjoyment until completed.

_____ _____ Spontaneity a key element.

_____ _____ Cooperation with others a key element.

_____ _____ Competition with others a key element.

_____ _____ Planning usually a key element.

_____ _____ Usually do in same general area.

_____ _____ Generally use same objects to participate.

_____ _____ Usually aware of time while participating.

_____ _____ Starting and stopping times usually known before participation begins.

_____ _____ Usually self-directed.

_____ _____ Usually directed by others.

_____ _____ Generally think of as pleasurable.

_____ _____ Money a primary consideration.

9. How do you feel about the relationship between work and play in your life?

   _____

   _____

10. Is a distinction made between work and play in your classroom(s)?
    _____ _____ If yes, how has this distinction been made?
    yes   no

    _____

    _____

11. Are there things to play with and things to work with in your class-room(s)? That is, is a distinction made between play things and work things? _____ _____ If so, list them below:
    yes   no

    work *things*   play *things*

12. Are opportunities given for play in your classroom(s) only if time allows or are they a part of the curriculum schedule?

    _____ if time allows _____ part of curriculum schedule

13. Work activities are usually

    _____ teacher directed _____ student directed
    Play activities are usually

    _____ teacher directed _____ student directed
14. Which activities do you think are more important?

    _____ work activities _____ play activities
15. Where does more student choice occur?

    _____ work activities _____ play activities
16. Are starting and stopping times more likely for

    _____ work activities? _____ play activities?
17. Do you tend to emphasize completing one's involvement in

    _____ work activities? _____ play activities?
18. You may wish to use a cassette recorder to tape children involved in work activities and play activities and then listen to yourself and students. You might think about the questions above while doing so, or you may center your attention on two questions:

How do I feel about my life with respect to work and play?

What am I teaching children and myself with respect to work and play and how can I reinforce those things I like and change those things I don't like?

In using Self-Inventory 3 with hundreds of teachers, a rather common response pattern has developed. Part of this pattern is outlined below:

Work	*Play*
Required and supervised by others.	Chosen by self.
Duty.	Fun.
Clear boundaries with respect to time (starting and stopping) and space (where it must take place).	Boundaries, if any, up to the participant(s).
Adultlike.	Childlike.
Limited expression.	Free expression.
Tension often associated with this.	Relaxing.

What is clear is that our culture and society have taught us that there is a distinction between work and play, a distinction that is reinforced by our language. At the same time, famous persons are sometimes praised for their sense of playfulness. It is interesting to read obituaries on this score. A famous historian was described as a no-nonsense son of one of Boston's famous families, but a famous architect was described as having the ability to create a line as playful and zesty as a Miró sketch. In trying to solve this dilemma, inservice teachers in a seminar suggested that one's attitude is the key factor in whether an activity is considered work or play. As one student remarked, "When a person is thoroughly immersed in something, it is play, for time and space are of little consequence." He added, "The person who is playing is completely connected to the process."

How do teachers perpetuate the distinction between work and play? One teacher commented, "I often tell the children to do their work and then we can go out and play." In saying this she demonstrated that she not only segmented time according to work time and play time but also distinguished between the classroom as a place where work occurred and the playground (note the name) as a place where play occurred. You may ask, "Doesn't it have to be this way?" Consider for a moment the teacher who helped her children learn the metric system by measuring the boundaries used in their ball game outside the school. Or note the physical education teacher who had a classroom presentation titled "Good eating can be fun!"

The relationship between work and play perceived by the teacher has a significant bearing on how the teacher feels about himself or herself as a person. A sense of playfulness is also obvious in the way the teacher feels about other people and the physical environment. The person who integrates work and play achieves a kind of balance that is absolutely essential to the centering process. New learnings are frequently the result of viewing existing situations from a new angle; a sense of playfulness makes this possible.

It is difficult to conclude this discussion of work and play without noting that some people enter both work and play with a "win or lose" attitude in nearly all situations: working one's way up the ladder at the office is a matter of defeating others in a series of confrontations, just as winning at tennis or bridge is what really counts. These "social Darwinists" provoke anxiety in others and in themselves for they see their relationship with others and the environment as a question of "survival of the fittest." They isolate or separate themselves from others and the environment, feeling that neither can be trusted, and they continually play a role designed to cover up their own weaknesses.

Cooperation and teamwork are what is really needed, for no one person can do everything that needs to be done. Such cooperation is based on recognizing and trusting others' abilities, but the social Darwinist is stuck in a game of his own making. He will often make effective starts on educational projects but his distrust of others prevents him from inviting those he really needs to finish the project.

Other educators are primarily interested in learning to do some things well at work and play, but they don't always try to win, nor do they think that others' "victories" are their own "defeats." They have learned to connect, rather than disconnect, and they know that trust and cooperation aid the growth and development of others and themselves. They have achieved kinship with others and oneness with their environment.

Conflict and Commitment

Thus far we have seen that being centered or feeling good about the "wonderful me" each of us has within depends on relating to one's feeling, thinking, and acting, and integrating work and play. A third characteristic of being centered focuses on how the teacher has learned to deal with conflict and commitment. Does the teacher squarely face the inevitability of conflict or skirt conflict by pretending it doesn't exist or by trying to be all things to all people? What kind of commitment does the teacher make in a given situation and is he or she conscious of the degree of commitment given in this situation? Self-Inventory 4 begins our investigation into these important issues.

SELF-INVENTORY 4

1. My family taught me to relate to conflict in the following ways:

_____

_____

_____

_____

My reaction to them at the time they handled conflict in these ways
was

_____

_____

_____

My present feeling about my family's reaction to conflict is

_____

_____

_____

and my teaching reflects this reaction in the following ways:

_____

_____

_____

2. My formal schooling taught me to relate to conflict in the following ways:

_____

_____

_____

_____

My reaction to formal schooling at the time it handled conflict in these ways was

_____

_____

My present feeling about my formal schooling's teaching about how to relate to conflict is

_____

_____

_____

and my teaching reflects this teaching in the following ways:

_____

_____

_____

Prospective and inservice teachers generally react to the self-inventory by saying that *their* teachers felt a good deal of discomfort when conflict existed in classrooms. Strongly voiced disagreements between two students in a classroom were occasionally entertained but such disagreement between a student and the teacher were almost nonexistent: the teacher used positional authority to head off or quickly stop such disagreements. When asked to explain this phenomenon, the prospective and inservice teachers usually cited their teachers' lack of experience in squarely facing and learning from conflict.

At the same time, the rhetoric surrounding our system of government in the United States suggests that it is healthy for conflict to exist between people with opposing views, between branches of the government, and between business, labor, and government. Such disagreement, it is argued, leads to improved conditions in all areas of a democracy. Furthermore, it is contended that our nation's schools prepare students for participation in a democracy. The irony is obvious!

Teachers bring different family experiences to the matter of relating to conflict. Many say that their families repressed conflict whenever possible while others indicate that their homes were veritable battlegrounds. If squarely facing conflict was a natural part of family life, they had to make adjustments in many formal educational settings where conflict was considered taboo.

Earlier in this chapter we recognized the importance of (1) being honest with oneself about one's feelings and (2) finding what one considers to be the best ways to express such feelings. When a person is centered enough to be honest about his or her feelings, it is natural that there will be perceived disagreements and conflict within oneself and with others. And it is also natural that expressing such feelings in what one considers to be the best way possible will at times produce conflict and disagreement with others. Where does this understanding lead us? It leads us to the question: *How much of my resources am I willing to commit in a particular situation in order to try to get what I think is worth getting?* Conflict and commitment are therefore intertwined.

Some people would have us believe that they are always *fully* committed to all of their objectives in a situation and they argue further that they will fight very hard in all situations in behalf of their values. If we spent some time with these people in a variety of situations, we would find that their contentions are simply not true. What we would discover is that their commitments would vary from setting to setting, which is to say that their support for particular values would not be constant, and within a setting their degree of commitment to particular objectives would also vary.

Think for a moment of four different settings in which you were a participant: for example, a faculty meeting, a classroom at a particular time, a social situation, a sports situation where you were a participant, or a meeting of a voluntary organization. Consider a particular objective you had in each of these settings. After examining the commitment scale which follows, indicate with the corresponding number the degree of commitment you had to the particular objective in the setting identified.

SELF-INVENTORY 5

Four Settings	One of My Objectives	Degree of Commitment

Commitment Scale[4]

1. I will sacrifice my life and/or the lives of my family and/or those I dearly love.
2. I will give up the respect of those whom I love and I'll forego my status and professional achievement.
3. I will forego economic security and my career.
4. I will have serious conflicts between what I think should be done and my reluctance to do it. I may have to alter my work style and give up those techniques which had previously been successful and beneficial and learn new ones.
5. I will have to alter some habits with which I'm quite comfortable, thus making my job somewhat more difficult. I will feel uncomfortable from time to time as I'll do things that don't seem to be the best way to do them based on past experience and present assumptions.
6. It doesn't make any difference, as past experience indicates. My choice, therefore, is between tweedledee and tweedledum.

The commitment scale demonstrates that one's stated values may be consistent with or at odds with one's behavior. The reader is being asked to look at the consequences of values acted upon in particular settings. The commitment scale also aids us in becoming more conscious of the internal conflict we feel when there is a discrepancy between stated and acted-upon values. It is also being argued that some conflict between values in one's value system is inevitable. To be centered is to make sense out of these mixed signals so that we feel a reasonable balance in relationships between values.

For example, an elementary school teacher values private (individual) expression in doing art work and at the same time she values children working and playing together. The teacher makes a number of decisions regarding curriculum and instructional settings in order to achieve a balance between opportunities for individual expression and cooperative expression. But it is the teacher as a professional who must make decisions which lead her to feel that her own value system has balance or is centered. Others can advise her but she must center herself by making her own choices. And she will achieve this by escalating on the commitment scale at some times in some situations and de-escalating on the scale at other times.

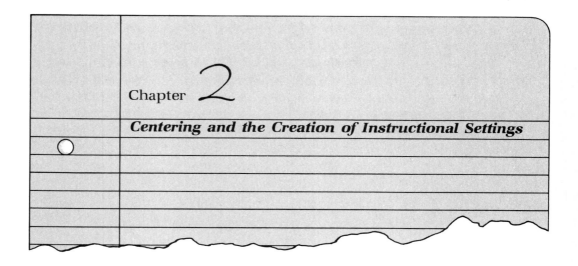

Chapter 2

Centering and the Creation of Instructional Settings

Each of us as a teacher works and plays in order to express a "wonderful me." This centering process gives vitality to our instructional leadership, and the process of becoming centered is a powerful influence on children and other participants in instructional settings. In the process of cooperatively building learning settings, we in turn are transformed and our vision of what the children, the setting, and ourselves can become gives us energy as people and educators. The vision also reminds us of the good feeling that comes from connecting rather than separating ourselves from others and the environment.

The remainder of this chapter consists of learning activities and suggestions for creating instructional settings that will help others, particularly children, participate in the centering process that frees one's "wonderful me." The materials are not programmed instruction in any sense. Rather, they are a compendium of suggestions based on the optimistic assumption that the teacher is an artist who gives shape to new experiences for children and in the process is also personally transformed.

Integrating Thinking, Feeling, and Acting

In chapter 1 the reader was asked to consider two guidelines for relating to feelings: (1) be honest with yourself as to your feelings; and (2) find what you consider to be the best way to express such feelings. The following lesson plan was designed to help children implement these guidelines.

LESSON 1   FEELING AND EXPRESSING ANGER

Objectives: As a result of this lesson, the student will:

(1) experience two situations, one where an adult transmits the feeling that it is okay to feel anger and the other where an adult transmits the feeling that the feeling of anger is unacceptable; and

(2) choose what he or she feels are acceptable ways to express anger.

Methods and Materials:

1. Ask the students to identify several situations they have experienced in the school where two students were angry about something. List the situations on the blackboard. For example, they might include:
   a. two students fought over the use of a crayon;
   b. two students bumped into each other in the hall;
   c. two students try to sit in the same chair at the same time.

2. Choose two students and have them sit in chairs in the middle of a large circle of students in chairs (or you may wish to have students sit on the floor). Ask two other students to sit next to the role players telling them that they will be listeners who will tell the rest of the class how their partners feel about the situations that follow.

3. Choose one of the situations from the board and have the two role players get into an argument. Then intervene as the teacher by saying: "You have *no right* to be angry and I want you to stop this argument right now." Ask the role players to tell their listeners their feelings in reaction to the teacher.

4. Choose another situation from the board and have the same two role players get into an argument. Then intervene as the teacher by saying: "You have *every right* to be angry but I want you to consider what you

think are the best ways to express this anger." Ask the role players to tell their listeners their feelings in reaction to the teacher.

5. Ask the listeners to tell the rest of the class what the feelings of the role players were in the two situations. Discuss the difference between being given the message that it is okay to feel anger as opposed to the message that it isn't okay to feel anger.

6. Ask students to consider possible ways to express anger in the two situations that were role played. Discuss the outlet each student would have chosen.

7. Bring in newspaper articles or have students bring in newspaper articles where people, groups, and countries feel and express their anger. Discuss the ways in which they expressed their anger, asking the students if they support such expressions.

Evaluation: Observe student responses during and after the role playing. Ask students to observe expressions of anger on television and identify those expressions they consider to be healthy and those they consider to be unhealthy.

Another lesson that teachers have found especially effective in helping students understand and express anger is titled "What Bugs You?"

LESSON 2   WHAT BUGS YOU?

Objectives: As a result of this lesson the student will be able to:

(1) express feelings about what "bugs" him or her;
(2) listen carefully to what "bugs" other students;
(3) give reasons why things bother people; and
(4) make decisions as to how to relate to himself or herself and others who are bothered by particular things.

Methods and Materials:

1. Ask the students to move their desks against the wall and place their chairs in one large circle.

2. Explain that "we are going to discuss things that 'bug' us."

3. Use the values clarification "whip" and begin the sentence "The thing that bugs me the most is . . ." and have each student who wishes an-

swer the question as it "whips" around the circle. Students who don't wish to respond for one reason or another can simply say "I pass."

4. Go to the board and write some of the reasons why certain things annoy us.

5. Return to the circle and use the incomplete sentence "A good way to deal with the thing that bugs me the most is . . ." using the values whip so that each student who wishes to can respond.

6. Give the students pieces of 12 in. by 18 in. drawing paper and have them draw a bug and write on it what bugs them the most. Put these on a bulletin board after they have been cut out and colored.

7. Sit in the large circle and informally discuss people in the news who bug students.

8. When a person is especially bugged by someone, place an empty chair in front of him or her and have the student speak to the chair as if the other person were sitting there and tell this person exactly what is so annoying.

9. Have the "bugged" student sit in the empty chair and answer the criticisms.

10. Ask the student how the two different roles felt. Ask for ways to better understand those who annoy you and vice versa.

Evaluation: Observe student responses and reactions during the discussion. At a later date, ask again if the student is bugged by something and if so what he or she has done about it.

One teacher describes her feelings after using the lesson plan "What Bugs You?"

I simply didn't realize how many pent-up, angry feelings my students had. And, it seems to me that they have a right to complain about what bugs them in most situations. One child who is short complained because cashiers frequently don't wait on him but instead wait on adults even though he is next in line. Other students had the same experience and found it extremely frustrating. Another student was simply tired of a younger brother who seemed to get all the attention while he got all the blame. I also found out that a lot of things in the school bug these students. They don't think, for example, that they should have to simply take what is on their plates in the cafeteria when teachers get choices as to what items they want. All in all I found the lesson to be an excellent safety valve.

Anger is but one of the many feelings each of us experiences. At other times we feel a sense of accomplishment or good feeling and thus invite ourselves to celebrate. Celebrations need not be boisterous affairs. They are frequently quiet times when we feel at one with the environment: Life itself is being celebrated, for example, as one silently observes a beautiful sunset. Other celebrations are shared with persons in particular settings. The following lesson plan was written in order to help students and ourselves relate to celebrations as expressions of feeling.

LESSON 3   CELEBRATIONS

Objectives: As a result of this lesson, the student will:

(1) define the concept "celebration";
(2) experience a celebration and relate this experience to others in the class; and
(3) describe the similarities and differences between quiet and boisterous celebrations.

Methods and Materials:

1. Mix a series of cards into a pile and ask each student who picks up a card to quickly express his or her feeling on reading the word. Include some of the following words as well as other words of your choice: "Birthday," "Party," "Picnic," "Wedding," "Baptism," and "Funeral."
2. Ask the students what all of these words have in common. (They will probably have a difficult time with the word "funeral" as they have been taught that a funeral is entirely sad and isn't a celebration of a life that has been shared with others as well. If so, leave out the word "funeral" for the moment.)
3. If the students don't "discover" the word "celebration" as a common element of all of the words, write it on the board and ask for a definition of the term.
4. Ask the students for examples of celebrations they have participated in and then say, "Do all celebrations have to be loud and boisterous?" If they aren't sure of what you mean, ask "Can one celebrate a beautiful sunset all alone?" or "Can one celebrate the beauty of a flower all alone?" Have students give examples of private, quiet celebrations in their own lives.
5. Ask the students if their class has experienced any celebrations together or if any student has quietly and privately celebrated anything in the classroom this year. Also, ask the students if they would like to suggest any celebrations the class might have during the year and say, "Can some

celebrations be planned whereas others must just happen?" Discuss this matter.

Evaluation: Observe student responses. Have each student bring to class an example from a magazine or newspaper of a celebration.

A fifth grade teacher was enthusiastic about the use of this lesson plan:

> There is so much problem solving in our workbooks. The celebrations lesson gave us a chance to express ourselves in a joyful way. Problems can be depressing! The children simply hadn't thought of celebrating alone without noise. I think it is important that new discoveries in the classroom and outside the classroom be thought of as celebrations. The idea of a funeral as a celebration of a life shared with others introduced a lot of discussion. John and Mike talked about how sad they were when their cat "Junior" died and they had a funeral service in the backyard. They said they celebrated when they discovered that they had buried a cat that looked just like "Junior" but wasn't. The idea of a funeral as a celebration is tough to teach. I'm not sure what I'll do with this next time, if anything.

In discussing celebrations, one child said, "Whenever I feel good about myself, I celebrate!" The following lesson plan resulted from this child's statement:

LESSON 4   MY OWN POSTAGE STAMP

Objectives: As a result of this lesson, students will be able to:

(1) identify and express positive feelings about themselves and their achievements; and
(2) listen to others in the class who take part in this same process.

Methods and Materials:

1. Ask students to imagine that each person has been asked to design a postage stamp that expresses positive personal feelings.
2. Explain that the stamp will have six equal areas with a symbol to be placed in each area. (Note that a symbol is a concrete expression of a more abstract idea.) The symbols should represent:
   a. A personal achievement of which you're proud;
   b. The main feeling this personal achievement gives you;

c. How a person you like reacted to your achievement;
d. An object that gives you personal happiness;
e. The feeling this object gives you; and
f. How a friend of your choice reacts to this object.

a)	d)
b)	e)
c)	f)

3. Have the students place their stamps on a large envelope and see if other students can guess what each symbol represents.

Evaluation: Observe student responses, reactions, and their stamps.

It is both flattering and an aid to one's self-concept to be called by name. The following lesson plans focus on our uniqueness as persons.

LESSON 5   WHAT IS YOUR NAME?

Objectives: As a result of this lesson, students should be able to:
(1) recognize that everybody has a first name;
(2) feel that his or her name is important;
(3) acknowledge that children and others use names to identify themselves;
(4) recognize that some children in the class and school share the same first names; and
(5) conclude that some people use their middle name in place of their first name when relating to others.

Methods and Materials:

1. Begin the lesson by writing your own first name on the board. Ask, "Does everyone have a first name?" Ask the students to give their first names. If some students share the same name, ask the class to give attention to this fact. Ask, "What kinds of problems might occur because two or more students in this class have the same first name?"
2. Ask the students if any of them use their middle names instead of their first names in relating to other people. Discuss this matter.
3. Begin the sentence "I feel good about my first name because . . ." and let each child finish the sentence.

Evaluation: Observe student responses during the exercise. Ask children to name the first names of their favorite television personalities and tell why they like these names.

LESSON 6 THE NAME GAME

Objectives: As a result of this lesson, students should be able to:

(1) discuss feelings people experience when stereotyped; and
(2) identify constructive ways of communicating verbally and nonverbally.

Methods and Materials:

1. Read the following story to the children:
Jackie sat under the green holly bush and covered her ears. She couldn't hear anything, but she was able to feel the prickly leaves of the holly pierce her skin on the back of her arms. She could see down the small hill through a tiny opening in the bushes. The boys and girls were running home because large drops of rain were beginning to fall. The swings were the only moving objects on the playground. Jackie uncovered her ears. "Jackie! J-A-C-K-I-E!" her mother called.
"Oh Mom, please stop yelling that name," Jackie thought.
Ever since that new boy moved into the neighborhood, everyone laughed and teased Jackie for having a boy's name. Tears rolled down Jackie's cheeks. How could her mom and dad do this to her—give her a boy's name! Mom stopped calling her. After several minutes of listening to the rain beat the leaves and smelling the damp earth, Jackie jumped up and ran home. Boy was she going to tell her mom how angry she was for having been given a boy's name. Then they would probably get to talk about this terrible mess she was in.

2. The following questions may help facilitate the discussion of the story.
   a. Do you feel that Jackie can be a girl's and a boy's name?
   b. How did Jackie feel when the children laughed at her name?
   c. What could Jackie have done when the children laughed at her name? What would you have done?
   d. Do you think that Jackie stayed upset about her name?
   e. How do you feel about your name?

Evaluation: Closely observe students' responses during the discussion. Identify the original meaning of each child's first name in the dictionary and ask each child how he or she feels about this original meaning. Have each child draw a picture of what his or her name feels like and discuss this meaning with the class.

LESSON 7   EACH OF US IS UNIQUE

Objectives: As a result of this lesson, students should be able to:

(1) give attention to the uniqueness of each person's voice;
(2) discriminate differences among voices;
(3) recognize their peers' voices; and
(4) relate the feeling that exists in hearing one's own voice.

Methods and Materials:

1. Ask the children if each of us has a special sound to his or her voice.
2. Ask the children to select several songs to sing. As each child sings he or she can walk around the room. You should record each student's singing voice with a cassette tape recorder.
3. Play back the tape and see if students can identify the different voices.
4. Blindfold one child and point to another child to speak and see if the blindfolded child can identify the speaking voice. Give each child a turn in playing the role of the blindfolded person.

Evaluation: Observe student responses. Play recordings of famous television personalities' voices and see if children can identify them.

We have often been told that there is no movement without friction and likewise there is no change without conflict and disagreement. When people are honest with themselves as to their feelings in a particular situation they have taken the first step in squarely facing conflict, for such honesty is in fact recognition of the inevitability of conflict as one of the kinds of relationships among people. The following experiences should aid the teacher in helping children face conflict.

LESSON 8   FACING CONFLICT

Objectives: As a result of this lesson, the student will:

(1) consider the generalization that all events have multiple causes (multiple causation);

(2) consider the idea that people associated with an event interpret what happens according to their own needs and priority of values;

(3) project what would happen if the student in the case and people in general squarely faced conflict as opposed to not facing it; and

(4) describe the feelings associated with facing conflict or not facing conflict.

Methods and Materials:

1. Announce to the class that a person who collects money at a theater box office, the cashier, has just charged an eleven-year-old student the adult rate of admission although the adult rate of admission is supposed to begin at age twelve. The class is to identify reasons for this mistake and react to the scene between the cashier and the eleven-year-old student.

2. Select two volunteers and assign them their roles: one as the cashier and the other as the student. Have them sit in two chairs that face each other in the middle of a large circle of students in chairs. Indicate to the role players that the cashier has just taken the student's money and has given change. The student realizes that an adult rate has been charged.

3. The first decision the student must make is whether or not he or she wishes to squarely face the conflict rather than overlook it. The second decision the student must make follows from a decision to face the conflict: *How should the student face the conflict or what should the student do in dealing with the conflict?* Discuss these two major questions and list alternatives. Ask each of the students in the class how each alternative would feel.

4. Ask the cashier how he or she would react to the student's choice of particular alternatives. This should lead to a discussion of multiple causation and the fact that people interpret what happens in a confrontation according to their own needs and points of view.

Evaluation: Observe student responses during the sociodrama and discussion. If possible bring in a guest who is a cashier or interview and record (cassette recorder) a theater representative regarding the subject of the case.

LESSON 9   WHY ME, TEACHER?

Objectives: As a result of this lesson, students should be able to:

(1) discuss constructive ways to deal with angry or hurt feelings; and
(2) gain insights into misunderstandings.

Methods and Materials:

1. Read the following story to the children:
   Thomas and Dan were building the biggest rocket you ever saw. "Boy, what a rocket! Bet nobody ever built a rocket this fine. I can't wait to show this to my teacher, Mrs. Jones," Thomas exclaimed. He turned to look for Mrs. Jones. Just as he leaned sideways he felt a bump on his left elbow. The rocket came tumbling down. Crash! "You tore up my rocket," yelled Dan. Mrs. Jones arrived and said to Thomas, "This is the third time I've spoken to you today about problems with blocks and I don't want you to play in the block area any more the rest of the week." Thomas had a lump in his throat. It was so big it hurt. He couldn't say anything. He left the blocks and sat in a corner in the book area. "How could Mrs. Jones ever understand that I had an accident and sometimes I just don't do things on purpose?" he said to himself.

2. The following questions may help you with the discussion that follows the story:
   a. Does this kind of thing happen to you at times? Tell us about it if you wish.
   b. Why didn't Thomas talk to his teacher about the problem?
   c. What are some ways that Thomas and Mrs. Jones could deal with their problem?
   d. When would be a good time for them to talk about their feelings?

Evaluation: Observe student responses. Role play a similar situation with the children and see if they apply what they've learned.

LESSON 10   DIVORCE

Objectives: As a result of this lesson, students should be able to:

(1) express their feelings verbally and nonverbally;
(2) demonstrate that they feel comfortable enough to share their similar experiences with the class; and
(3) better understand their own feelings.

Methods and Materials:

1. Read the following story to the children:

   Kim stretched to look out the window. She could still see the back of Dad's car with its left red light blinking. Soon it was out of sight. She plopped down on the sofa. Suddenly her tummy felt tight and it hurt. She missed Dad. She got her Weebles treehouse out of the closet and sat by the fireplace in the den to play. Oops! Mr. Weebles fell out of his house. Oh well! Kim thought about how she and Mom and Dad had always sat by the fireplace and had pizza and coke. Gee, that was nice. Dad always wanted lots and lots of salt on his pizza. Kim jumped up and carried her Weebles treehouse back to her room and put it in the closet. She ran to the kitchen.

   "Mom! Why did Dad have to leave?"

   "Because Dad and I always got into fusses and it was too difficult after a while to work out all the problems," said Mom. "Did I do anything to lead to this divorce?" Kim said to herself. She added, "I wonder if I should live with Mom or Dad?"

2. The following discussion question may help you with this lesson:

   a. Why did Kim's parents get a divorce?
   b. Do all parents who fuss at each other a lot need to get a divorce?
   c. How did Kim feel about the divorce?
   d. Will her feelings change as she gets older?
   e. Is it natural for a child like Kim to think that she did something to cause the divorce? Was it really Kim who caused the divorce? What would you say to Kim about this if she were your best friend?

Evaluation: Observe student responses during the discussion. Bring a guest to class who works with people (adults and children) who are experiencing divorce in the family and see what questions the children ask this person.

Conflict resolution is a very important process in instructional settings, as new teachers quickly discover. Covenants or agreements are formed between participants in the classroom although we aren't even conscious of many of them. Covenants lead to more predictable behavior which lends security to people in the setting. Much of the conflict children experience occurs outside the classroom, for example in the halls, the cafeteria, and the playground. Rules and responsibilities therefore become an important part of the "hidden curriculum" in elementary schools, the curriculum that isn't obvious as one looks at teachers' lesson plans or curriculum guides.

All of us recognize the importance of guidelines and rules for our lives and at the same time we usually sense the fairness of such rules if we know the reasons for their existence. That is, the reasons need to have a basis in fact. Dishonest scare tactics are frightening to younger children and recognized as dishonest by older children. For example, a kindergarten teacher told her children that they should get in line quickly and get out of the building during a fire drill or the fire might jump down their throats.

When teachers take the time to have children discover the reasons for particular rules, they often experience rich dividends. A second grade teacher who was at her wits' end because of the behavior of some of her children, tried to have them react to a case or story since her early efforts of yelling at the children failed: "I really used the case approach as one more attempt to 'civilize the little animals' but it turned out to be more a review of known facts in a more interesting and personal way—a way that helped all of us get a little peace for awhile."

She began the lesson by saying that "we've had a lot of shoving and pushing lately. Jorge and Jesse were real angry with each other when we came into the room because they had been thumping each other. Do you have any idea why boys and girls shove each other when they get together?"

JOY: Because they want to get ahead of the other guy.

JORGE: That's right! Jesse pushed me to get ahead of me.

JESSE: He pushed me! He started it! He's always pushing and he comes up in back of you and chokes you with his arms.

MICHAEL: Then they bump you after being pushed and you bump the next person. Somebody could get hurt!

TEACHER: How should we deal with this then?

ELEANOR: We should have lines if we can't go quietly to the cafeteria and playground.

TIMMY: If someone doesn't behave in line he can go to the end of the line.

TEACHER: Do your parents stand in line sometimes?

REGINA: My mother stands in line when she buys groceries.

ELEANOR: We stand in line when we go out of church.

MICHAEL: Sometimes we stand in line like eggs in a carton but sometimes we're like sardines in a can!

TEACHER: Let's see if we can go quietly to the cafeteria and playground, but if we can't let's go like eggs in a carton.

The example the teacher sets in facing conflict when children have to be disciplined influences the tone of the classroom. An elementary teacher describes how she used a different approach to discipline in order to have her students be honest with themselves as to their feelings and express such feelings in an instructional setting:

George was in a mean, ugly mood again—this time between the language arts block and lunch. He cornered Tom, his favorite target, in the hall and yelled, "You stole my magic marker!" Tom wasn't going to take anything from George. He responded with equal force, "You're crazy, George." He added, "Ease off or I'll come upside your head!" With this reaction George got the first swing in and the hall fight was on. A student called me to the scene and I got the boys apart although they were so emotional that they looked like they were ready to kill each other. I was so tired of this conflict and George in particular that I had had it. It seemed that nothing had worked.

I decided to use a technique that I had recently seen demonstrated at an inservice workshop. It was designed to let students immediately release their emotions in a tense situation and see other points of view than their own. I asked my friend from across the hall to keep an eye on the rest of my class and I took Tom and George into an empty classroom. "Tom," I said, "You can walk around the back of the room or sit down but I want you to be quiet." Then I turned to George and asked him to come to the front of the room with me and help me do some things with the empty chairs. By this time the two boys, although still plenty mad, were curious as to what was going on.

I pushed the chairs out of the way and left only one in a large space. "Tom," I said, "Pretend that George is in that empty chair." I pushed another empty chair opposite the other one and said to Tom, "Pretend this was George before the fight and tell him what you said." Tom said, "I don't want to." I sat in George's chair and told Tom, "I'm George, and so tell me what you said to him before the fight." Tom said, "I didn't take your magic marker!" Since Tom didn't have anything else to say I asked George to come to the front of the room and Tom went to the back of the room. George was now in the spirit of things and said, "Tom, you stole my magic marker." He added, "You take a lot of my things when I'm not looking and I don't like it." I asked Tom to join George in the front of the room with each in a chair and they really started yelling at each other. Tom said, "I'm tired of your picking on me all the time and you'd better square away or I'm going to come upside your head."

I then placed a chair next to George and asked him to imagine his mother in it. "George," I said, "Sit in this chair and say what your mother would say to you two boys." He talked in moderate tones and tried to stop the conflict in a rational way. Next I took a chance and asked the boys to place an empty chair where they thought I, their teacher, would sit. The boys placed my chair way away from them. George sat in the chair as the teacher and was obviously ineffective in dealing with the conflict. (This was something I talked to the boys about in the next few days and they said that I hadn't given them enough attention.)

I had now spent about fifteen minutes with the boys and our class had to go to lunch. The boys seemed to have cooled off and released their feelings. In fact, Tom had his arm around George when the boys sat on the rug in story time. The next day George came to my desk and said that he didn't really have a magic marker the day before and he wanted me to know it. I thanked him for his honesty. This role playing experience opened up a new world for me and I began to find some things out about my students and me that I hadn't known before.

The teacher in this episode gained new perspective on herself by understanding how she was viewed by two of her students.

Discovering New Relationships Between Work and Play

Before discussing new relationships between work and play, it will be useful to evaluate conceptions of work and play presently held by children. A variety of activities such as the following can be used to accomplish this goal:

1. Tell the students that they will be asked to draw two pictures: one will demonstrate what they mean by the word "work" and the other what they mean by the word "play." Then have each child tell other students what his picture means.

2. Use a values "whip" whereby you start a sentence and each student who wishes completes the sentence. Responses will "whip" around the circle with those who wish to abstain saying "I pass." Sentence 1: "When I say work I mean . . ." Sentence 2: "When I say play I mean . . ." Discuss the profile of responses by listing them on the board after the exercise.
3. Ask each student to bring to class two objects for "show and tell": one represents his or her idea of work and the other represents his or her idea of play. Discuss student responses.
4. Ask each student to bring to class a picture from a magazine or newspaper that represents work and a second picture that represents play.
5. Ask each student to write a brief essay entitled "Work and Play in the School."

Teachers who have used these pre-evaluation techniques have discovered student responses that reflect our culture's imperatives. The general profile is one of separation of work and play in our thinking both with respect to time and space. The language children use to describe this separation of work and play illustrates and perpetuates the separation itself:

- When I go home after school I'm supposed to do my homework and then I can play.
- My mommy works during the day.
- I wish my dad were home more. He works all the time selling cars.
- Can we play on the playground today or do we have to stay inside in our classroom because of the drizzle?
- If I get my workbook lesson done, can I go over to the reading center?

The following lesson plans were written in order to discover new relationships between work and play.

LESSON 11   GOING WITH THE FLOW

Objectives: As a result of this lesson, the child should recognize that:
(1) there is a constant sense of playfulness, motion, growth, and change in living organisms, including human beings, for we wiggle, grow, and change;

(2) this change and growth and flow of things are inevitable and can't be stopped and to try to stop these processes produces anxiety and tension in the person who tries to do so; and

(3) the person can try to redirect the flow of change and is sometimes successful in doing so.

Methods and Materials:

1. Bring a plant to class and watch its growth for several days with each child describing this growth with comments in a daily log.

2. Have the children observe a nearby creek and/or show slides, a filmstrip, or a movie to demonstrate the flow of water. (Children are especially interested in water projects such as dams.)

3. Ask the children how they have learned to understand change and growth in their own lives. (Examples they often give are scales, birthdays, and height measurements—often marked on the edge of a bedroom door.)

4. Ask the children what they, plants, and moving water have in common. (You may eventually summarize in part by saying that all are living, changing organisms with *organisms* defined the students' own words.)

5. Ask the students to draw pictures of living organisms of their choice. Ask, "Is it really possible to capture the wiggles, flow, growth, and change of living organisms in a picture or work of art?" (This question usually provokes a good deal of discussion, with students generally concluding that a picture or work of art can never really change like a living organism but it can try to capture this change. As one student said, "Some pictures do this better than others!")

6. Ask students if we can accurately identify this change, growth, wiggling, and flowing as a kind of playfulness. Discuss their responses at some length.

7. Ask students if one can stop the change and growth in living organisms. Add, "Do you know anyone who has tried to do so and what happened to them and the organism in the process?" See if students think that tension and anxiety are the result of such efforts. For example, "What would happen if you tried to push a plant back into the ground to keep it from growing?" Ask, "Can a plant's growth be *redirected* in this manner or by placing it at a different angle to the sun?" Ask, "Can the same thing be done to a stream of water?" Then ask, "Is success guaranteed if one tries to redirect the growth of a living organism?"

Evaluation: Observe student responses. Ask students to bring to class pictures of growing organisms from magazines or books and discuss what they personally observe as well.

LESSON 12   IMMERSING ONESELF IN AN ACTIVITY

Objectives: As a result of this lesson, the student should analyze the view that:

(1) one's attitude toward an activity largely determines whether one calls this experience "work" or "play"; and

(2) completely involving oneself in an experience leads one to lose track of time and this kind of experience is difficult to label as "work" or "play."

Methods and Materials:

1. Place the following items in a large cardboard box in front of the room so that students can't see what the objects are: a hoe, a rake, a tennis racket, a pocket calculator, and a book.

2. Ask a student to come to the front of the room to remove one item from the box and identify it as a work item or a play item. Continue this process until all items are removed from the box.

3. Ask the following questions if they haven't been discussed already:

    a. Are a hoe and rake viewed differently by a full-time gardener and a weekend gardener? If so, in what ways?

    b. Is a tennis racket viewed differently by a tennis pro and a weekend "hacker"? If so, in what ways?

    c. Is a pocket calculator viewed differently by an accountant and a child using it for scorekeeping during a card game? If so, in what ways?

    d. Is a book viewed differently by its author and the reader? If so, in what ways?

    e. Does a person sometimes view the use of each of these items as work and sometimes as play? Discuss this matter.

4. Ask the students, "If you are completely involved or immersed in something, what happens or how do you feel?" (See if students discuss the fact that one loses track of time. If not, discuss this idea with them.)

    a. Ask, "Can one easily identify something as 'work' or 'play' if a person is completely involved in an activity?" Discuss this as there is not a "right" or "wrong" answer.

Evaluation: Observe student responses. Ask students to bring in newspaper and magazine articles that treat this subject. Have students interview adults they know on this subject, using cassette recorders if possible.

Career education is a response to many factors in contemporary society including the desire for more meaningful work opportunities. The role of today's woman in our nation is another issue that must be considered in career education. It is commonly accepted that traditional treatment of careers by schools has been sex-biased, with women excluded from some vocations and men excluded from other vocations. Past efforts in career education have also largely been antiseptic with participants in various occupations always happy and helpful. (How difficult it was for many of us when postal employees first involved themselves in strikes! How could the friendly mailman do that to us!)

It is easy to assume what children know and think and feel about various occupations, but we are frequently mistaken. For this reason, teachers are wise to begin their lessons on career education by finding out what students presently think with respect to different careers. The question "What job would you like to have and why?" is a good starting place as the following responses from first graders reveal:

PETER: I would like to be a doctor because you can take care of people. You can take care of the "inside of people." It is fun to work in a hospital and I sometimes make believe I'm there. My sister plays nurse. A nurse is a doctor's helper. (Author's comment: the implication is that the nurse isn't a professional in his or her own right.) I'm going to be a doctor because they get more money than anyone else.

JANET: I want to be a stewardess because you can serve food and wash the dishes and do what you should. I wanted to be a pilot but it's too hard for me. (Author's note: talk to flight attendants or watch them and you'll discover a job that taxes one's resources.)

DAVID: I want to be a bus driver because I like to drive. I like to take people places, too. And I like the pay. And when I get back with the money I would buy my mother a fur coat.

FRED: When I grow up I want to be a policeman because I like to help people and I'm strong. I am not bad. I am good. (Author's comment: it is a rude awakening when a child discovers that some police are involved in corrupt practices.)

DONNA: I want to be a teacher because I like to learn about teachers. We like to play school. I like school. I'm in a good class and I like my teacher.

HARRY: When I grow up I want to be an astronaut or a man who fills out taxpayers.

JAMES: I want to be a lifeguard so I can save people and watch little kids play in the water.

JANE: When I grow up I want to be a nurse so I can give shots not get them.

Another way to evaluate what students already know about careers is to ask them what careers adults they know have. The responses that follow were given by first graders in answer to this question:

CARLOS: My father fixes cars.

ANDREW: My uncle is a milkman.

CAROLYN: My mother babysits.

SYLVIA: My father cuts grass and fixes trees for people.

JAMES: My mother goes to school. She's going to be a teacher.

ROBERT: I have a friend who cuts hair.

BUCK: My daddy is a policeman in a car.

FERNANDO: My father drives a garbage truck.

EDWARD: My mother makes plastic things. I don't know where she works.

FRANCINE: My mother is a nurse's aide.

CHRISTINA: My mother works in a bank.

GRISELDA: My mother works in a drive-in and gives food to people.

The teacher in Los Angeles who used this exercise in her class said, "The other children didn't say anything and knew little about occupations although two children said they knew that their fathers gave their mothers money for taking care of the children."

This teacher wanted the children to address the question, "What will your being in school have to do with the kind of job you choose?" Her first graders answered:

JOSE: If you go to school you learn a lot and you know how to do things better.

CHRISTINA: My mother says that if you go to school a long time you can get a job that pays you a lot of money.

The children's comments mirrored the most common responses children have given with regard to the relationship between schooling and career success: the more formal schooling you have the more prestigious the job you'll have and the more money you'll make, thus assuring yourself happiness.

Career choice was the subject of a lesson plan in the introduction to this book. The plan was titled *Vocations*. The following lesson plan complements the earlier plan.

LESSON 13   CAREER EDUCATION

Objectives: As a result of this lesson, the students will be able to:

(1) identify different careers;

(2) consider the careers they might enter;

(3) demonstrate their understanding of the interdependence of careers; and

(4) define "cultural imperative" as a command or order issued by one's culture or way of life and discuss the cultural imperative that a person should have one career all of his or her life.[5]

Methods and Materials:

1. Have pictures of men and women "on the job" and ask:
   a. What is the job or task being done? (Introduce the concept "career" if possible by having the students suggest it as a synonym for job or vocation or occupation.
   b. How do these people depend on other people who have other jobs? (For example, the assembly line worker in the automobile plant depends on those who make car parts and those who will sell the cars.) Write the concept *interdependence* on the blackboard.

2. Ask each student to write one or more careers on a card and then you can read all of the careers to the class.

3. Ask the children which careers they think they would like to have and why. Each child should draw a picture of what he or she would look like on the job.

4. Ask the children if they expect to have one career all their lives. Ask them what others expect of them in this regard. Ask them the advantages and disadvantages of changing jobs or careers.
   a. Introduce the concept "culture" as meaning "way of life."
   b. Introduce the concept "imperative" as meaning command or order and remind them of how the word is punctuated in our language. That is, with an exclamation point.
   c. See if the children conclude that our culture naturally gives us certain commands with regard to careers and that we still, how-

ever, can choose to disagree with such commands. Explain that all cultures have their own imperatives.

5. Ask students if they would like to interview adults about their careers using cassette recorders where possible, after which the tapes will be played back to the entire class. Discuss what should be included in the interview. That is, what kinds of questions should be asked?

Evaluation: Observation of student responses.

Bring in a guest and see what questions children ask about his or her career.

Distribute career brochures and have children identify biases (for example, sex biases) in the pictures and writing.

The next two lesson plans also relate to career education.

LESSON 14   CAREERS AND JOBS

Objectives: As a result of this lesson, students should be able to:

(1) identify the distinction between careers and jobs;

(2) define "career clusters"; and

(3) place appropriate jobs under the correct career cluster.

Methods and Materials:

1. Discuss the difference between a career and a job. For example, education would be a career whereas a teacher, principal, aide, supervisor, professor, and superintendent would be jobs within this career.

2. List the following career clusters on the board and discuss possible jobs within each cluster:

   a. Agribusiness and Natural Resources

   b. Business and Office

   c. Communications and Media

   d. Marketing and Distribution

   e. Construction

   f. Manufacturing

   g. Transportation

   h. Fine Arts and Humanities

   i. Public Service

   j. Consumer and Homemaking

   k. Health

  l. Hospitality and Recreation
  m. Personal Service
  n. Environmental Control
  o. Marine Science

3. Using the following list of jobs, have students categorize these under the proper career cluster:

banker	veterinarian	clerk
reporter	insurance agent	secretary
farmer	conservationist	homemaker
disc jockey	plumber	computer operator
realtor	brick mason	lab technician
accountant	railway engineer	actor
textile worker	beautician	sanitarian
truck driver	oceanographer	dispatcher
firefighter	forest ranger	writer
cashier	hotel manager	contractor
babysitter	advertising agent	fisherman
travel agent	electrician	furniture producer
broadcaster	interior designer	painter
dentist	artist	pitcher
aviator	minister	teacher
service station owner		

4. Ask students to freely associate anything that comes to mind when you read the following to them: farmer, realtor, minister, teacher, and banker.

  a. Discuss career stereotypes illustrated in this activity. Discuss how stereotypes are "useful" and harmful.

Evaluation: Observe student responses, particularly during the free association activity. Have students bring to class literature about different careers and jobs and identify career stereotypes and job stereotypes supported by the literature.

LESSON 15 CAREER SYMBOLS

Objectives: As a result of this lesson, students should be able to:

(1) define the term "symbol"; and
(2) identify symbols associated with some careers.

Methods and Materials:

1. Bring to class a large trunk of various symbols that represent various fine arts careers: paint brush, ballet shoes, comedy-tragedy masks, sheet music, etc.
2. Ask the student what each item represents and discuss whether these items are considered masculine or feminine and discuss cultural and sexual biases.

Evaluation: Have children bring to class symbols from other careers and discuss what they symbolize.

Technological advances, prolonged life, and the development of retirement complexes have recently raised our consciousness as to the importance of the wise use of leisure time. A growing body of literature on work and occupations has also made us aware of the discontent many feel in their vocations. A natural response on the part of the discontented is to turn to avocations or hobbies for a more satisfying life. Schools have probably done a good deal in stimulating interest in hobbies such as athletics and voluntary organization activity, although this interest has been part of the "hidden curriculum" and will therefore not be found in lesson plan books and accreditation reports. The following lesson plan serves as a springboard for learning more about the use of leisure time.

LESSON 16   USE OF LEISURE TIME

Objectives: As a result of this lesson, the student should be able to:

(1) define what is meant by "leisure time";
(2) discuss, share, and communicate his ideas about hobbies and leisure time activities; and
(3) creatively and actively demonstrate his understanding of others' hobbies by pantomiming such leisure time activities.

Methods and Materials:

1. Introduce the lesson with a puppet you have made: "Hello. Do you know who I am? My name is Holly Hobby because I love hobbies. They're so much fun. Do you know what a hobby is? Who knows what the word "leisure" means? What is "leisure time"?

2. Continue question and discussion time with some of the following questions aiding you:
   a. Does anyone know somebody who has an interesting hobby that we haven't talked about? Have any student who is interested in doing so, pantomime this hobby with the other students guessing what the hobby is. You may wish to ask students to do this pantomime as a pair or small group.
   b. Why did you choose the hobbies you have? Where do you do this hobby? Does your hobby help you relax? Do you think about time when you do your hobby or do you usually "forget the clock"?
   c. What hobbies do you think you might be interested in as a result of our discussion? How much would this hobby probably cost you?
3. Tell the students about your hobbies and the hobbies your friends enjoy. Discuss how people at different times in their lives tend to like different hobbies although there is no one age for a particular hobby.
4. Discuss retirement complexes, using literature from such places. (You may wish to discuss cost of living in such a complex with older students.)
5. Students may wish to visit a retirement complex.
6. A guest or small group of retired citizens may visit your classroom. Planning for their visit, including building interview questions, can be a valuable experience for the students.
7. Have students bring to class articles and pictures from magazines and newspapers on retirement conditions in our country. Class discussion can follow.
8. An excellent experience for children is to join a "Mobile Meals" team that takes meals to older citizens in the community.
9. Students may wish to use a cassette recorder to interview retired citizens after which their interviews can be played back to the class.
10. You may wish to have a parents' organization meeting devoted to "the wise use of leisure time" with students playing an active part in this meeting. Posters students have made could be shown at this meeting. And a cassette recording could be played.
11. Have guests into your class with each person talking about his or her unusual hobby.

Evaluation: Observe student responses in the activities above. Ask students to make their own puppets who will talk about their hobbies. Ask students to bring their favorite hobby to class if they can or else bring a picture of it.

SUGGESTED ACTIVITIES

1. Have students read excerpts from famous persons' autobiographies or biographies in which their views of work and play are discussed.
2. Ask students to bring to class works of art, for example, pictures and paintings, that they find playful.
3. Have guests from the creative arts as speakers in your class. Students may wish to interview the guests which would give students the opportunity to construct appropriate questions.
4. Invite students to write a brief play on the subject of "work and play." Present the play to another room or rooms or perhaps to the entire school.
5. Explore the importance of humor in integrating work and play. Excerpts from Mark Twain, for example, are illustrative.
6. Ask students to look at comic strips, such as "Peanuts," to see what their creators say about work and play.
7. Ask students to view their favorite television programs to analyze relationships between work and play.
8. Write three words, *Heroes*, *Villains*, and *Fools*, at the top of the blackboard with an empty column beneath each. Have students identify famous persons under each column head and discuss implications for the relationship between work and play.

Learning About Conflict and Commitment

In order to face conflict, the person must decide his or her level of commitment in a particular situation. It seems of special importance that the child understand that commitment and accepting responsibility aren't simply difficult, demanding, obligatory processes. They also provide the opportunity for learning, sharing, and growing, as the following lesson plan demonstrates:

LESSON 17   COMMITMENT AND THE ACCEPTANCE OF RESPONSIBILITY

Objectives: As a result of this lesson, the student should be able to:

(1) define *commitment* and *responsibility;*

(2) recognize what is involved in being the main person responsible for the care of others; and

(3) weigh alternative ways for meeting one's own needs and the needs of others in relation to agreed upon covenants.

Methods and Materials:

1. Read the following case or story to the children:

   Jody is eleven years old and has a four-year-old brother named Tim. Jody's father is at work and her mother has gone on some errands for several hours. She has promised to pay Jody two dollars for taking care of Tim and drying the dishes. About ten minutes after her mother leaves, the doorbell rings. It is Jody's best friend Jane who wants Jody to come out and play.

2. The following are some of the questions you may wish to ask:

   a. Should Jody go out of the house with Tim in order to play with Jane? Why or why not?

   b. Should Jody invite Jane in to play in the house? Why or why not?

   c. If Jane is invited in, should she get part of the two dollars Jody's mother will pay for baby-sitting?

   d. While doing the dishes, Jody breaks a glass. Should she tell her mother? What should Jody do if she can't find the vacuum cleaner to pick up all of the tiny bits of glass?

   e. Should Jody's two dollars be used to pay for the glass?

   f. What does it mean to have the responsibility for the care of a small child?

3. Write *commitment* and *responsibility* on the blackboard and ask the children to tell what they mean.

Evaluation: Observe student responses. Have a mother as a guest and have her explain what she expects of a babysitter. Have a few of the children interview parents with cassette recorders on the topic of responsibility and play back the recordings in class. Then discuss them. Ask the children to describe their "chores" or responsibilities at home and list them on the board.

Students who were asked to discuss their "chores" at home responded as follows in their first grade classroom:

JOY: I help my mother at the grocery store sometimes and I help cook the food and set the table.

CYNTHIA: I pick up my toys at home so my brother and sister don't trip over them.

VICTOR: My mom sews for people and sometimes my shirt gets torn or a button comes off and I take it home and try to fix it so she won't have to.

RACHEL: My mom gets mad at me if I don't work and she hits me and makes me go to bed. She needs help 'cause there are lots of kids and they get things messed up and are too little to clean up.

VICTOR: I do stuff for exercise too. I work in the yard. I rake and water and mow the yard some and help keep the yard clean.

DEANA: I use the vacuum at home.

JORGE: I take out the garbage.

BUDDY: I wash the dishes all the time.

WILLIAM: I wash dishes all the time and then I clean the kitchen and wash the floor.

JESÚS: I help my dad in the yard and go to work with him on Saturday and learn how to do iron work.

JAMES: I hate to do work at home but if I do it quick then I can get out and play.

What did the first grade teacher learn from the discussion of responsibility (chores) at home?

I mainly wanted the children to understand the reasons for doing chores at home. Most of the children in my class this year are from low-income homes and so there was no question of pay or allowance for few get any allowance or get paid for chores. They sometimes get pay for extra work, however. Money for spending is usually from birthday presents or from a relative.

Most of the children had a very realistic attitude toward chores already for they face real situations where their work is essential. They took pride in telling about their work. I was happy to hear that!

A few did work only to avoid punishment, but even they knew why they must essentially do the work. There was only one student who said she didn't do chores.

One of the best parts of this lesson was that each child discovered that every other child also had responsibility at home. It was good for me to find out more about the children's homes and their relationships with parents and others at home.

If I teach this lesson again, and I will, I want to try to have the children learn the idea of "interdependence." They learn big ideas in math and I think they can in other areas of the curriculum too. The idea that we are all interdependent is so important in explaining how we get along with others.

Most of us have probably tried to build a lemonade stand at some time in our young lives. An elementary teacher capitalized on this interest to teach about responsibility and commitment.

LESSON 18 THE LEMONADE STAND

Objectives: As a result of this lesson the student should:

(1) be able to describe what is involved in accepting responsibility;
(2) be able to define advertising;
(3) describe what safety measures are involved in relating to others and the physical environment; and
(4) be able to make decisions about what is fair with regard to paying persons involved in labor, in this case, with their lemonade stand.

Methods and Materials:

1. Read the following story to the children and ask some of the questions included:

   It was one of the hottest days yet, that summer day, when David, who is eight years old, and his younger brother Mark, who is six years old, decided they wanted to set up a lemonade stand. They lived in a section of town where a lot of cars drove past their home. Not only that, but there was a golf course behind their house and one block away there were men working on a new house. The boys knew they would have a lot of business. It was still early in the morning and the boys were very excited over their idea of setting up a stand. They had been awake much of the night thinking about it.

   a. Should the children ask their parents' permission before setting up the stand? Why or why not?

   They did ask their mother and she agreed it would be a good experience for them but that they would have to get all the necessary things together on their own as she was going to have a very busy day herself.

   b. What things do the children need before selling lemonade? For example, what is lemonade made of and do they need any kind of table or stand?

   c. How much of the materials will they need? How much money will they need to buy the materials? Should they ask their mother to loan them some money? Why or why not?

d. How can they persuade their mother to go to the store with them to buy what they need?

The children thought about what they should use as glasses or cups and couldn't decide at first.

e. Should they use paper cups? Glasses? Why? The boys remembered that they needed to get people's attention in order to sell their lemonade. "It pays to advertise," said David.

f. What is advertising?

g. How could the children advertise?

Mark had the idea for a sign:

COME WET YOUR WHISTLE
FRESH LEMONADE 5¢ A CUP

Mark ran into the house and got a large brown paper bag, a black crayon, and some tape. David then printed very large letters on the bag and they taped the sign to the front of the card table. The boys were set! They sat very patiently for a long time as cars passed but didn't stop. Just a few neighborhood children stopped to buy lemonade. David decided that he would take a walk to see if the men were working on the new house.

h. Should he tell his mother?

David told his mother and she said it was fine if he was careful.

i. Should Mark go along too? Why or why not?

Mark stayed at the lemonade stand and David left. David was pleased to find out that all the workmen wanted a cup of lemonade but said they couldn't take time to go to the lemonade stand.

j. Should David say that he and Mark will bring the lemonade to the new house?

David put six cups in a small cardboard box and took the lemonade to the workmen. Fortunately, he remembered to take some change with him. In the meantime, Mark got the idea of taking lemonade to the golf course and moved the lemonade stand to the backyard near the golf course.

k. What safety hazards did Mark have to consider?

Mark and David had heard their father tell them of the dangers of flying golf balls that sometimes even landed in the backyard. So David and Mark moved the stand back some from the course. No sooner had they done this than some nice golfers stopped by for lemonade. It wasn't long before the boys had to go inside and make another batch of lemonade.

l. Now that the day was nearly over and the boys had earned $2.50, how should they decide who would get how much money? Should they divide the money or should David get more since he is older? (Indicate to the children that one of the most important questions in any business is to try to decide what fair share of money should be paid to each worker. Introduce the term "equitable" and see if the children understand that it means fairness in relating to people.)

Evaluation: Observe student responses. Have students write an essay on "What I've Learned from the Lemonade Stand Story."

An important concern of educators and parents is the safety of children. Parents of very young children can't be with them all of the time. Children are taught rules and guidelines for crossing the street and other safety related activities after which they must simply learn to accept responsibility for their own actions. Learning experiences on the subject of safety therefore provide us with an excellent opportunity to create settings in which children learn to be responsible for their own behavior.

A good place to start in relating to safety is diagnosing what children already know about the subject. The following lesson plan serves this purpose.

LESSON 19   WHAT DO YOU KNOW ABOUT SAFETY?

Objectives: As a result of this lesson, students should be able to:

(1) construct safety posters and explain the meaning of them to classmates and students in another class;
(2) identify ways in which students might bring the attention of others to safety hazards at home and at school and suggest ways to eliminate such hazards; and
(3) communicate with parents and other adults about safety.

Methods and Materials:

1. Introduce the idea of constructing safety posters to another teacher and students in the class and have students begin constructing posters. Your introduction may be aided by using a "values whip" with students answering the following questions while seated in a large circle. (Follow

a sequence around the circle but explain that a student can say "I pass" if he or she doesn't have a ready answer.)

    a. The biggest safety problem at home is . . .

    b. The biggest safety problem at school is . . .

2. Have each student explain the meaning of his or her poster to others in the class.
3. Have half of your class members meet with half of the other class that is doing posters, with each student explaining his or her poster.
4. If propitious, have the rest of the students who haven't met with each other from the two classes do the same thing.
5. If possible have parents engage in a similar activity on a parent night after which you show them student posters and have a discussion of safety at home and at school.
6. Discuss with students ways in which they can use their poster ideas at home and at school.

Evaluation: Observe student responses. Use an audio recorder to record student responses from the other class or parent responses to ideas in no. 6 above. Play back the responses to your class and continue your discussion. If possible, have students react to parents' posters.

After diagnosing children's present knowledge and attitudes toward safety, you may wish to use cases or incidents in order to stimulate further discussion about safety. The following lesson serves as an example.

LESSON 20   REACTING TO SAFETY HAZARDS

Objectives: As a result of this lesson, students should be able to:

(1) give reasons for the accident experienced by the girl in the story read by the teacher or another student;
(2) suggest ways in which the bad accident could have been prevented;
(3) list accidents students have experienced themselves or heard about at home and at school;
(4) give reasons for such accidents and suggest ways in which they could have been prevented.
(5) involve themselves in school activities that will correct hazards at home and at school.

Methods and Materials:

1. Read or have a student read the following story to the class:
   A third grade student's father stored his house painting equipment, including paint, in his workshop-garage. There was an old wood stove that he used during the winter to keep the workshop warm. One February evening the workshop-garage caught fire and the fire department put out the fire with water from their trucks. The next day before school, Susan rode her bike that she got for Christmas in the alley by the workshop, slipped and fell into the broken lumber and paint equipment, and broke a leg and scraped her arms and back severely.

2. Begin the discussion by asking the following questions:
   a. What are some reasons for the accident?
   b. How might it have been prevented or kept from happening?
   c. Could accidents like this have happened near your home? At school? Explain in detail.
   d. How might we prevent such accidents? For example, could we make safety posters to be placed in the halls of the school? (If posters have already been done, what could we do with them? Place them in supermarkets, churches, libraries, laundries?) Could we write a newsletter for adults and students to read? How should we communicate with the principal about our ideas?

Evaluation: Observe student responses. Bring safety posters from industries to class and see if students can identify reasons for such posters and the meaning of each poster.

As children get older, they hear about the responsibilities of being a citizen of the community, the nation, and the world. The following lesson plan was written in order to introduce the idea of wider responsibility to the children.

LESSON 21 RESPONSIBILITY OF A CITIZEN

Objectives: As a result of this lesson students should be able to:

(1) communicate their feelings about the responsibility of being a citizen;
(2) make decisions about involvement in other people's problems; and
(3) make decisions about what they consider to be "better," "worse," "right," and "wrong" in particular situations.

Methods and Materials:

1. Set the stage for role playing by reading the students the following story: Jane and Alice, both twelve-year-olds, have just left the store and are walking toward Jane's mother's car in the parking lot. As they walk toward the car they see a car back out of a parking space and ram into the side of a parked car. Instead of stopping, the car hurriedly leaves the parking lot. Jane and Alice saw the driver of the car and were able to get the number of the license plate.

2. Assign students to role play the situation: one as Jane, a second as Alice, a third as the driver of the car, and a fourth as the mother of Jane. Try to get students to convey the real feelings of the person in the role.

3. Ask the question, "Would it have made any difference if Jane and Alice had seen Jane's mother's car hit?" Why or why not?

4. Ask the students to give a brief description or definition of citizenship.

5. Go to the board and write "rights" in one column and "responsibilities" in another column. Then list under each what students tell you.

6. Count off 1,2,3 with an equal number of students in each group and have group 1 identify the rights and responsibilities of a citizen of the city, group 2 the rights and responsibilities of a citizen of the state, and group 3 the rights and responsibilities of a citizen of the nation. Discuss their findings as a total class.

7. Ask the whole class to discuss the rights and responsibilities of a citizen of the world.

8. Ask the students if there is a "right" and "wrong" answer to difficult situations as opposed to "better" and "worse" answers. Discuss this matter.

Evaluation: Observe student responses. Ask students to identify other problem situations they might encounter as citizens.

Conclusion

Part One was written for two major purposes: to help each of us see the "wonderful me" within him or her by honestly relating to feelings in particular situations and choosing the best way(s) to express such feelings; and to suggest springboard activities to implement our "wonderful mes" in instructional settings. Both purposes are based on the assumption that the teacher must be an effective, growing learner in order to be an effective, growing teacher of children in our elementary schools. In Part Two we will see how our relationships with others in organizations are influenced by our culture and society, and how we as teachers and our children can benefit from such understandings.

NOTES

1. For an excellent discussion of centering, see M. C. Richards, *Centering in Pottery, Poetry, and the Person* (Middletown, Conn.: Wesleyan University Press, 1964).

2. See Gail Sheehy, *Passages* (New York: Bantam, 1977).

3. A stimulating general source on networks is Seymour Sarason, *Human Services and Resource Networks* (San Francisco: Jossey-Bass, 1977).

4. Dale L. Brubaker and Roland H. Nelson, Jr., *Creative Survival in Educational Bureaucracies* (Berkeley: McCutchan, 1974), p. 102.

5. Seymour Sarason describes this as the "one life—one career imperative" in his book, *Work, Aging and Social Change* (New York: The Free Press, 1977).

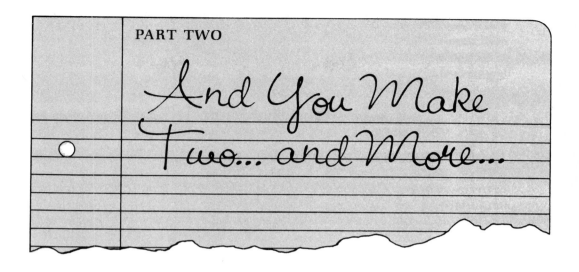

PART TWO

And You Make Two... and More...

In the previous part it was argued that each of us has a "wonderful me" within and that this positive self can be nourished by being honest with oneself as to one's feelings in a particular situation and choosing the best ways to express such feelings. The title of Part Two supports the view that one's relationship with others can lead to a psychological sense of community which in turn enhances the dignity of the person. The format of this part is like that of the first.

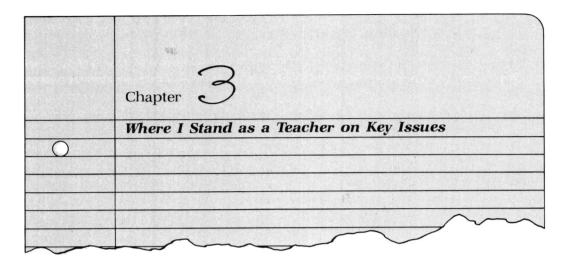

Chapter *3*

Where I Stand as a Teacher on Key Issues

Most of our great-grandparents and grandparents would be shocked in encountering societal changes created in large measure by our Technetronic Age, a period of time marked by technical and electronic inventions. Before considering this era, react to the following self-inventory, which focuses on products and processes that have emerged in the last quarter century or so.

SELF-INVENTORY 6

If you have experienced the following, what were your feelings at the time? If you have not experienced the following, how might you feel if you did?

1. You are asked to roll your thumb across an ink pad and then leave your thumb print on a paper form in order to cash a check at a large store.

Your reaction: _____

_____

_____

2. A rotating closed-circuit television camera points toward you as you try on shoes in a shoe store.

   Your reaction: _____

   _____

   _____

3. You are asked to write your student identification number twenty-two times in filling out university computer cards.

   Your reaction: _____

   _____

   _____

4. You are asked to punch information into a computer while registering for university courses thus saving you an hour which you would otherwise have spent waiting in line.

   Your reaction: _____

   _____

   _____

5. After listening to your doctor, a general practitioner, and receiving a bill for his services, you take his advice and make an appointment to visit a specialist.

   Your reaction: _____

   _____

   _____

6. You need a lawnmower and have a choice from among thirty models at three different large stores.

   Your reaction: _____

   _____

   _____

7. You take a camping trip into the mountains and sleep little because many campers play battery-operated television sets, record players, and radios most of the night.

   Your reaction: _____

   _____

   _____

8. You spend a weekend with a friend whose family has a television set in each bedroom, the family room, and the kitchen.

   Your reaction: _____

   _____

   _____

9. You use your new stereo component parts to build a stereo that sounds much better and costs much less than the one your dad and mom bought fifteen years ago.

   Your reaction: _____

   _____

   _____

10. You can leave a nearby city and fly in a jet plane to Europe in three to five hours.

    Your reaction: _____

    _____

    _____

11. You can use a telephone to immediately call a friend or member of your family in another country.

    Your reaction: _____

    _____

    _____

12. Electronic surveillance equipment is openly advertised in a magazine so that its purchasers are encouraged to listen to others without their knowledge or consent.

Your reaction: _____

_____

_____

13. You visit a supermarket and can't touch fruit and vegetables for they are packaged in plastic.

Your reaction: _____

_____

_____

14. Someone gives you a microwave oven.

Your reaction: _____

_____

_____

15. Approximately one-fourth of the people in your neighborhood move away from the neighborhood each year.

Your reaction: _____

_____

_____

16. You want a new house, furniture, and so on, and can get these things cheaper because there are so many other ones like them.

Your reaction: _____

_____

_____

17. Due to vandalism in your school, a school board member makes a motion to construct a high fence around the school grounds, a fence that will be locked each night just after the students leave school for the day.

Your reaction: _____

_____

_____

Teachers who used the self-inventory led us to an inescapable conclusion: any technical advance has both advantages and disadvantages, which is to say that it solves some problems and creates others. The following summary of common responses to the self-inventory demonstrates the ambivalence people experience in today's industrially advanced societies:

1. Electronic surveillance equipment is appreciated by those citizens who don't break the law by stealing, for they feel that prices will be lower if thieves are discouraged or caught; yet, they feel some anger when they are under surveillance in a store and tremendous anger when the surveillance equipment is used illegally (Items 1, 2, and 12). They really object to the fact that a few who break the law cause others to suffer (Items 12 and 17).

2. All respondents found bureaucratic red tape, such as writing identification numbers repeatedly, evoked anger and boredom (Items 3 and 5). Many were proud that they had learned to "beat the system." For example, some said that they went directly to the specialist, thus bypassing the general practitioner or internist (Item 5). At the same time, all respondents supported innovations that saved time in their professional lives (Item 4). There was ambivalence with respect to leisure-time innovations, for some gadgets challenged traditional values (Items 7, 8, 13, 14, and 16).

3. Technetronic discoveries were appreciated in one sense for providing us with more choices, often at lower prices (Items 9 and 16). However, respondents often felt that we may label as "overchoice," the state of being overwhelmed by too many choices (Items 6 and 14).

4. Noise pollution and invasion of one's privacy were definite drawbacks of the Technetronic Age, according to respondents (Items 7, 8, and 10). All appreciated opportunities for their own quick transportation and communication in the event of need. (Items 4, 10, and 11). They felt fearful, insecure, sad, and lonely when those dear to them "overused" these opportunities (Items 10 and 15).

5. Standardization was considered an advantage in that it made products

more predictable, accessible, and cheaper, but a disadvantage, according to some, in that others would know this fact and use it to their advantage. There is no prestige in this reality (Items 6, 7, 8, 9, 14, and 16). Standardization sometimes limits the use of one's senses ("You can't squeeze the tomatoes"), and can also hide flaws (Items 6, 13, and 16.).

We will now consider how the realities of our Technetronic Age influence one's need for a psychological sense of community, a major dimension of elementary school learning.

Attitudes Toward the Community

Each of us has the need to experience a psychological sense of community. This occurs when one has a mutually supportive network of dependable relationships in contrast to sustained feelings of loneliness.[1] As with many other things in life, one realizes the importance of a psychological sense of community by its absence. A major characteristic of a psychological sense of community is its members' voluntary or willing identification with some overarching or encompassing values, values that members feel might be lost if not defended and nurtured.[2] Before saying more about our entering into various communities, let us identify and examine present attitudes toward the topic itself.

SELF-INVENTORY 7

1. What communities do you identify with or feel are a part of your life?

_____

_____

2. What are the characteristics of these communities?

_____

_____

_____

3. Do you feel that all communities share some or all of these characteristics? Why or why not?

_____

_____

_____

4. Quickly list any thought or feeling that comes to you in hearing the following words:

   compact: _____

   covenant: _____

   contract: _____

5. Which of these words above (one or more) best describes the relationship you would like to have with:

   a school board: _____ superintendent: _____

   a principal: _____ parents: _____

   other teachers in the school: _____

   students in your classroom: _____

6. In what ways have teachers you've known tried to build a classroom community?

_____

_____

7. In what ways have administrators you've known tried to build communities in the school?

_____

_____

8. Please list relationships in your life that are:

intense and enduring: _____

_____

not very intense but enduring: _____

_____

intense but brief: _____

_____

not very intense but brief: _____

_____

9. Which of these four kinds of relationships do you prefer to have with:

school board members: _____

the superintendent of your school system: _____

curriculum supervisors: _____

the principal in your school: _____

teachers in your school: _____

parents of children in your classroom: _____

children in your classroom: _____

the school's custodian(s): _____

cafeteria workers: _____

10. In what ways, if any, have advances in transportation, communication, and the electronics field in general influenced your answers to Item 9 above?

_____

_____

_____

Those who have responded to the self-inventory have generally been concerned with what has happened to the person's sense of community as a result of the many fast-moving, far-reaching changes stimulated by technological advances in our society.[3] Teachers cite a simple index for such change: the turnover of students in their classrooms due to parents moving from one area of the country to another.

What is the term preferred by teachers to describe the relationships they want in schools? Apparently the term "compact" is too antiquated as some respondents referred to the "Mayflower Compact" as the only instance of the use of the word. "Contract" was considered useful in a legal context but left respondents with a cold formal feeling in the school setting. There was overwhelming support for the term "covenant." Although there was agreement that the term "covenant" should be used in describing school relationships, respondents felt that the more bureaucratic and formal word "contract" more accurately described their relationship with the board of education and superintendent of schools. Let us now turn to two dimensions of covenants, their intensity and duration, as they influence the teacher's psychological sense of community.

Intense and enduring covenants are rare indeed according to those who used the self-inventory. Such covenants are usually reserved for family and friends. And yet, our discussions with respondents indicated that advertisers have used technetronic advances to promise us intense and enduring covenants when we buy their products: cars, airline tickets, vacation tours, houses, toothpaste, and hair products serve as examples. We are left with the feeling that our money will buy something, usually plastic, that will assure us of close relationships with other people. Electronic products, such as stereo systems, television sets, and radios, are advertised as "friends" who will keep us from being lonely.

Respondents said they want intense and enduring covenants with children in their classrooms. One teacher added, "We often have to make up for what is missing in a child's home." Another teacher wrote, "Some of my children come from homes where adults are seldom there and when they are they don't relate to their children." Ironically, however, few teachers felt that their principals deliberately or consciously tried to build a sense of community in their schools. A key to this dilemma may have been provided by one respondent who said, "Our principal is so busy with details that she spends little time with anything else." Many principals probably reflect the values of the larger school culture as they perceive them: the principal should be a manager rather than an educational leader who is concerned with something as "esoteric" as building a psychological sense of community in the school.

Intense but short-lived covenants can have a profound influence on the teacher. "When a supervisor from central office comes into my classroom," one teacher remarked, "I'm a different person." She continued, "The supervisor's office is in the central office building and I know that a good word to those higher up can help me and a bad word can really hurt me." For this teacher, the supervisor represented a bureaucratic superior, an authority figure in a structured hierarchy rather than a professional colleague who could be related to in a lateral way. Since most organizations are bureaucratic, the teacher has had a lifetime of experience in relating to bureaucratic "superiors" and "inferiors." Visits to the dentist, being called into the boss's office, giving a speech, flying in airplanes, and other similar activities were cited as examples of intense but short-lived relationships in our society.

Not very intense but enduring covenants become rituals. Teachers referred to such things as taking attendance, collecting lunch money, and other record-keeping activities. Teachers meetings were also mentioned as enduring rituals where nothing much happens. A respondent described how she relates to such rituals: "I just throw it into 'automatic pilot' and put my mind into neutral." A brief description of this ritual captures the spirit of low intensity—enduring settings:

> Five minutes before the meeting was scheduled to begin teachers and aides began to come into the library. Many had their arms full of teaching materials, lesson plan books, and lunch bags. Since it was early in the morning most weren't fully awake yet. At 7:40 A.M. the meeting began with the principal making two or three brief announcements. One teacher asked questions about the size of paper that should be used for the bicycle safety poster contest and who the judges would be. A second teacher asked questions about entertainment for parents at the next P.T.A. meeting.

Another teacher recommended that a good old-fashioned play be given by the second graders.

Throughout this discussion faculty members and aides were busy with a number of activities. Three teachers were writing lesson plans. One aide used a magic marker to trace outlines of turkeys on a piece of brown paper. One teacher used scissors to cut egg cartons into small pieces for bulletin board decoration. Another read a children's book. One teacher ate crackers and sipped a coke to fight off morning sickness. And the librarian placed reinforcing glue on book spines. In spite of their activities, all listened to the discussion and even entered into it at times.

Not very intense and short-lived covenants are probably the most common relationships we have with others. One teacher related, "So much of the time I pass and repass people." She added, "It doesn't cost me anything really and we're pleasant to each other most of the time." Shopping was the most often cited example of this kind of covenant: one feels at home in stores previously frequented and yet store clerks don't tax your emotional resources. Relationships between teachers and parents are often considered to be brief rituals that aren't too demanding. "Meet your child's teacher night" is an example of such a ritual.

Now that we have identified and discussed four kinds of covenants, what significance does this have for one's psychological sense of community? First, the four kinds of covenants make us conscious of the relationships we have with others in life in general and schools in particular. This awareness should lead us to the conclusion that we need many different kinds of relationships with other people, which is to say that no one kind of covenant is possible or desirable at all times in all places. For example, in spite of our rhetoric or the rhetoric of some others, it is impossible to sustain intense enduring covenants with everyone we meet, for we simply don't have the resources to do so. At the other extreme, we feel a deep sense of loneliness and alienation if we always relate to others superficially and briefly.

This leads us to a second conclusion from our study of the four kinds of covenants: each of us makes important decisions about how we will use our resources, which is another way of saying that the kinds of relationships or covenants we choose to enter into affect our psychological sense of community with respect to both quality and quantity of contacts. *Each of us can make a difference in creating a psychological sense of community in our lives in general and in our schools and classrooms in particular.* It is this realization that gives us personal and political potency: we realize that we have the resources to influence others and in the process learn more about ourselves. In order to meet this challenge, it is necessary to better understand our culture and the organizations within it, for both culture and organizations serve the purposes of constraining us (trying to maintain boundaries) and liberating us by giving us something to react to and work and play through. Covenant formation and community formation are therefore inextricably related to culture and organizations.

Cultural Influences

The assimilation of culture is a lifelong process that teaches us what is worth knowing and valuing. This process is frequently so subtle that we aren't even aware of what we have been taught. It is often in visiting another culture that we experience "strange" feelings about our own culture and the other culture. Upon disembarking from his ship in another country, a young serviceman looked about him and said to his buddy, "Have you ever seen so many foreigners?" The following self-inventory will launch us into a discussion of how our culture has influenced us.

SELF-INVENTORY 8

1. What evidence of cultural influence do you see in the classroom you experience?

2. In what ways has our culture influenced us through language?

3. How do school traditions that you can identify reflect cultural imperatives (commands)?

_____

_____

_____

4. What myths surrounding schools and schooling exist and how do these myths represent cultural imperatives?

_____

_____

_____

_____

_____

5. What symbols exist in your school and classroom and how do these symbols represent cultural imperatives?

_____

_____

_____

_____

Difficulties in defining "culture" are many, as experienced by those of us who have sat through "Culture and Personality" courses without ever settling on a definition. Anthropologist Dorothy Lee defined culture as "a system which stems from and expresses something had, the basic values of society."[4] Elementary school children quickly grasp culture defined as "the values expressed in our way of life," when examples are given. It takes time, however, for children to work and play their way through deeper meanings of culture and cultural imperatives. When teachers have responded to the self-inventory above, they have had some difficulty because they haven't used a framework with its various elements (symbols, myths, traditions, and so on) for making sense of cultural influences.

A simple and unquestioned example of a cultural imperative that influences school and classroom architecture is the ninety-degree-angle corner. Nearly all rooms in schools have four ninety-degree-angle corners. A curvilinear structure would more faithfully represent the wiggles and playfulness of nature, such as trees bounced about by the wind, and yet none of this is apparent in school architecture in most school districts. Fortunately, many elementary school teachers build in their own wiggles and playfulness by bringing in old furniture, rugs, and other miscellaneous items.

The language of our culture is perpetuated by schooling processes, thus keeping alive myths of the culture. For example, most of us were taught that "our skin *protects* us from the environment" rather than "our skin *connects* us with the environment." What is a person's role in relating to the environment? One must learn to be aggressive and hard working (not playful) in order to win (overcome obstacles, often in the form of others who are also aggressive in their pursuit of victory). Grades, the currency of the schools, are symbols of this myth for they teach us that the product (getting a good grade) is more important than the learning process, arriving at the destination is more important than experiencing the journey. Good grades in school get you into a good college or university, *and if* you get good grades in a college or university you will get a good job, *and if* you get a good job you'll get good promotions, more money, more prestige, and so on. A product in the future will make all of this worthwhile, it is argued.

Other myths that support cultural imperatives are:

1. What one does in school (schooling) is learning.
2. The best learners get the best grades and the worst learners get the worst grades.
3. Teachers teach and students learn.
4. Students learn best in efficient classrooms and schools.
5. Educational innovations are more likely to succeed in new physical settings, such as new schools.
6. Students should be taught appropriate skills, such as reading, writing, and arithmetic, in order to engage themselves in one career for the remainder of their lives.[5]

Traditions in a school and classroom lend a sense of security and stability to the educational setting. The student knows that announcements will be made at a certain time of the day, lunch money will be collected first thing in the morning, and roll will be taken at the same time. Tradition also dictates that there will be a room for teachers in the building and this room will be better equipped than a room, if one exists, for aides, custodians, and others. (In one school, teachers were in an uproar because they were asked to give up their room in exchange for the aides' room. The aides needed a quiet room for typing and mimeographing, for their noise was disrupting children in the media center which adjoined the aides' "old" room.)

Organizational Influences

We have given a disproportionate amount of attention in our culture to the psychology of individuals as compared to the psychological growth of organizations. Parents have traditionally turned to Dr. Spock or some other child-rearing book when confronted with physical and emotional problems experienced by their children. It is only in recent years that our culture has given attention to the emotional health of organizations and it is still true that this emphasis pales in comparison to the number of articles, books, and television programs devoted to personal growth. Much of our naiveté in this regard is due to the myth that good people who enter into change processes as individuals will then naturally change the organizations of which they are a part. But time and time again we hear about changed individuals returning to their organizations only to be swallowed up by such organizations, which have a life of their own.

The teacher who wants to have better relationships with others in school communities would do well to begin by understanding how the school functions as an organization.

The following self-inventory should serve as well in getting us started with our inquiry into the school as an organization.

SELF-INVENTORY 9

1. Please list the main functions you think schools perform.

   _____

   _____

   _____

2. Identify two nonschool organizations and answer the question, "Do these organizations share the functions I've listed for schools?" Then ask, "Why or why not?"

   _____

   _____

   _____

3. Do you believe that the greater the influence of government on an organization the more bureaucratic the organization will be? Why or why not?

   _____

   _____

4. Do schools prepare students to function in bureaucratic organizations? If so, how is this done? If not, explain why not.

   _____

   _____

   _____

5. Do schools necessarily confine, indoctrinate, sort, and train students? If so, how is this done? If not, explain. What other organizations conduct or carry out the same functions?

Let us begin our discussion by noting that all organizations have a bureaucratic element in them, which is to say that some parts of their operations are structured hierarchically with "superiors" giving orders or commands to those below them on the organizational ladder. We are therefore left with the question "What is the nature (kind) and extent (quantity) of bureaucracy in an organization and what is the nature and extent of nonbureaucratic elements in an organization?" For example, some schools are organized according to bureaucratic lines for all school matters: the superintendent gives commands to the principal who gives commands to the teachers who give commands to the students. Other schools have a considerable professional element in them so that teachers decide matters such as scheduling, the organization of the staff (for example, in teaching teams), inservice education, and the use of space for instructional purposes. When professional decisions are made they are of a more collegial nature so that communication is lateral or horizontal rather than vertical.[6]

We will now identify and discuss functions schools perform for students.[7] It should be quickly added that schools vary as to the intensity and nature of each function as it is performed. And, it is also true that all organizations perform the first four functions to some degree in some way.

Confinement simply means that a person has to be in a certain place for a specified period of time regardless of his personal wishes with respect to being there. Various forces assure the school of performing the confinement function. State law, for example, requires the student to be in school for a given number of days, usually 180, and to attend between the ages of five or six to sixteen or eighteen. Teachers are also accountable in certain ways for the child's safety and the child isn't allowed to leave school grounds during the school day unless under the supervision of a school official. A good deal of flexibility still remains within the confinement guidelines if the teacher is defined primarily as a professional rather than a bureaucrat. But the confinement function will invariably be carried out in some way to some extent in schools.

Training is aimed at having students acquire those skills and modes of behavior consistent with the role of successful student. Skills may be categorized into four major areas: reading, writing, speaking, and modes of thinking. Some elementary teachers don't integrate subject areas, such as language arts, reading, and social studies, in training students to acquire skills, while other teachers do. Once again, the degree of emphasis given to training skills and the kind of emphasis given to training skills vary from teacher to teacher and school to school.

Indoctrination is the third major function that schools perform for students. It means that people are influenced to behave as you want them to behave without even questioning whether or not this is the way they want to behave or should behave. One way this is done is to fill the student's day with so many activities that there is little time to ask questions about the framework in which he or she is operating. Many, if not most, students know that grades and learning can be very different things and yet they are so busy trying to get good grades that there is little if any time to question the grading system. What is the student indoctrinated to believe? He or she is indoctrinated to believe the myths associated with schooling, myths mentioned earlier in this chapter. For example, the student is taught that education and learning result from schooling and those who attend school longer are better educated than those who drop out early. And they are taught that successful students become successful adult citizens.

Sorting leads to the kind of classification desired by the social system, in this case the school. The power that accompanies sorting is evident in the following questions: Is aspirin a drug or not? Is organized baseball a business, profession, or leisure activity? Is a person who is ten percent black and ninety percent white classified as a Negro or a Caucasian? In elementary schools we sort according to reading levels and abilities as we perceive them in a variety of subject areas. Who should play first chair trombone in the elementary school band? is a question that demonstrates how sorting occurs throughout the overt and hidden curriculum.

Providing the conditions for personal or self-development is the fifth function performed by schools. Much of our educational rhetoric surrounds this function: "We help the child develop his or her individual talents in order to be a creative member of our society." The difficulty with this fifth function is that it doesn't lend itself to easy evaluative procedures for it emphasizes process more than product and processes are more difficult to quantify than products. For example, a creative theme of the student's choice is harder to grade than a spelling test. For this reason, schools provide the conditions for personal or self-development largely in the hidden curriculum and the emerging curriculum. Spontaneous events in the classroom, the hallway, the playground, the stage, the media center and the like give the student more space and time for personal expression.

How have prospective and inservice teachers reacted to the self-inventory on organizational influences? They have felt uncomfortable with the terms "confinement," "indoctrination," and "sorting" and to a somewhat lesser extent with the word "training." But after some reflection they admit that these functions are performed by schools in spite of public relations rhetoric. And they agree that the fifth function, providing the conditions for personal or self-development, is largely carried out in informal settings from interest centers to playground activities. In light of this new consciousness, respondents agree that schools do train students to be good bureaucrats, particularly high schools and colleges and universities. At the same time, respondents point out that all organizations perform the first four functions and most organizations give less attention to the fifth function than does the school.

In concluding this discussion of the importance of organizations to teachers, other educators, and students, it is important to note that one's attitude toward one's own abilities and authority in general are related to one's relationship with organizations. For example, if I see myself as a capable person with many choices to make about my present and future, I am really saying that I have authority in myself: "I have a wonderful me within me!" But, if I don't see this authority in myself I must then lean on others who I feel are always more competent, which is to say that I will be an excellent bureaucrat who will always choose to obey orders or commands from other "superiors." Our challenge as elementary school educators is obvious and so the theme for this book: *We must find ways to help create learning settings that help others and ourselves to recognize our present talents and capabilities, which in turn will serve as the foundation for further growth and development.*

Chapter 4

Creating Settings for Learning About Cultures, Organizations, and Communities

In the beginning of Part Two, you were asked to consider various points of view as to the importance of cultural and organizational influences that affect the kinds of communities we form. These communities provide each of us with the opportunity to stretch, grow, and share with others and ourselves in order to fulfill in some way the best within us. Here are teaching experiences and lesson plans designed to help you implement instructional settings of your choice.

The Need for Community

Each of us has a psychological need to feel part of a community. The psychological sense of community gives us emotional security which in turn stimulates us to try out new ideas in a relatively secure environment. Being part of a community gives us the feeling that we belong: others accept us for who we are and what we do. The following lesson plan introduces elementary school students to the concept of community.

LESSON 22   BELONGING TO A COMMUNITY

Objectives: As a result of this lesson the students will be able to:

(1) define the concept "community";
(2) identify communities to which they belong;
(3) give reasons for belonging to a community; and
(4) identify ways to help others feel they belong to a community (issue positive invitations).

Methods and Materials:

1. Ask the students if they know what the concept "community" means, write tentative definitions on the board, and agree on a working definition for the class, such as "two or more persons sharing common interests and goals for a period of time."

2. List on the board communities to which students belong, their reasons for belonging to a community, and how it feels to belong to a community and not to belong to a community that they wish to join. Four columns on the board will cover these categories.

3. Discuss what "feeling alone" is like. Ask, "Can you feel alone even when you're with people?" "For example, do you sometimes feel alone at a party?" "Why?"

4. Then ask, "How can you react or relate to lonely feelings in various settings?"

5. Have each student draw a picture of "What my family as a community means to me." Emphasize that not all families have a mother and father, sisters, and brothers. Ask the students to define "family."

6. Ask the students to write a story on the topic "What it feels like to be a new student in the school." Then ask, "What can each of us in our school and class communities do to help a new student feel less lonely and more a part of the class and school?"

   a. You may wish to have students role play the story.

7. Ask students to read about early immigrants to the United States and discuss why they left communities in other countries to come to the United States and how they joined communities in the United States. If possible have students interview people who came to the United States and play back cassette recordings of the interviews.

Evaluation: Observe student responses. Have the class meet with another class and explain what they have learned.

The following lesson plan elaborates on the theme of immigrants to the United States and their need for a sense of community.

LESSON 23   IMMIGRANTS

Objectives: As a result of this lesson the students should be able to:

(1) describe how nonacceptance by a community works against people's need for community;

(2) relate how it feels to be unaccepted by a community; and

(3) discuss how most people react to such nonacceptance.

Methods and Materials:

1. Divide the class into groups of three or four students, leaving a small group of students unattached to any group. (You should probably choose strong leaders to be unattached.)

2. Each group will be put to work on a task such as practicing an unfamiliar group of vocabulary words with each student in the group participating. The task is not important and could be anything a small group could work on independently.

3. Each group will be told quietly by the teacher that they are not to let anyone into their group unless the outsider can do whatever they are doing better than they can.

4. The unattached students then should be told to go to a group and try to join it.

5. After the activity has continued long enough for the students to get the idea, a discussion should be held. Possible questions are:

   a. How did it feel to be left out of a group or community?

   b. How did it feel to exclude people from a community?

   c. Did anyone experience a problem in telling someone they liked that they could not join the group?

   d. Do communities in our school sometimes exclude others? How?

   e. Does our classroom community sometimes exclude others? How?

   f. Do communities within our classroom sometimes exclude others? How?

   g. What can be done to help include others rather than exclude them?

   h. Do other communities that you are familiar with exclude others? On what basis? Have you personally experienced this and if so

how did it feel? Have you personally excluded others and if so
how did it feel?

6. If appropriate to the learning level of the class, introduce the concept
"boundary maintenance" as a way communities try to include and regu-
late persons. The analogy of a tennis court with its lines (boundaries)
may be used.

   a. Ask students for examples of ways in which communities they
   know about maintain boundaries.

Evaluation: Observe student responses. Read excerpts from accounts of immigrants to the United States and see if students can apply what
they've learned to these case studies.

Several of us were involved in a prolonged discussion at a recent
education convention, the topic of the discussion being what should be
taught about prejudice, stereotypes, preferential treatment, and the like.
All of the discussants had been involved in building teaching materials
that focus on relations among whites, blacks, browns, American Indians,
and others. After some disagreement about minor issues, all of us agreed
that certain themes were common, in fact basic, to teaching about relationships between persons and groups. The extent to which the person
or community views differences and diversity as important to growth
rather than a threat to existence was considered to be the key issue.
"How should the teacher relate to this issue?" we asked. We were also
unanimous in our answer to the question: "We must create learning
situations in which all within them feel free to express where they presently stand after which we make choices as to how to weigh alternatives
for examining such stands. And then," it was added, "we must act out
such alternatives to see how we feel about them in practice." (You will
recall our earlier statement that *each of us must be honest with ourselves
as to our feelings in a situation after which we must choose how to express such feelings.)*

One place to begin to create learning settings where all within them
feel free to express feelings about community is with the following lesson
plan on "ins" and "outs."

LESSON 24   "INS" AND "OUTS"

Objectives: As a result of this lesson students should be able to:

(1) identify and discuss attitudes or feelings of "ins" toward "outs" and vice
versa with the "ins" usually (a) afraid of losing what they have, (b) feel-

ing a need to protect what they have, (c) distrusting the "outs," and (d) relying on force, command of the language, use of the media, etc. in order to keep the power they have, and the "outs" often feeling desperate, hostile, afraid, and detached even when they sometimes build their own community in response to the "in" community; and

(2) suggest and act out ways to relate to the "in" and "out" distinction that focus on tolerance for differences and diversity.

Methods and Materials:

1. Divide the class into two groups equal in number and tell one group "you have it" and the other group "you don't have it." (Students will ask you what *it* is but you should simply say "You know, you simply have it or you don't.")

2. Stand back and see what happens. You may have to act as a catalyst if nothing happens by saying things such as "Don't you want it?" Have groups reverse roles after what you consider to be an appropriate period of time.

3. After a period of time, write feelings of the "ins" and "outs" on the board and discuss what happened.

4. Now lead the discussion to the question, "What are ways in which communities can view differences and diversity as important for their growth rather than threats to their existence?" Also ask, "What does your answer to the previous question say about the allocation or use of resources, such as emotional energy, money, and expertise?" (They should see that it takes considerable resources to maintain boundaries in an "in" versus "out" situation and resources can be reallocated to better goals if diversity and differences are entertained.)

Evaluation: Ask students for examples of what they've experienced in this lesson from the school and communities outside the school. Observe student responses.

A Milwaukee, Wisconsin, first grade teacher adjusted the "ins" and "outs" lesson plan for her purposes as described in her own words:

I tried the lesson plan on "in" and "out" groups. We had never chosen teams before so the class was anxious to do this for a line soccer game to be played in the gym. I asked seven students to leave the classroom and wait in the hall for a minute. When they returned the two captains began choosing teams and the excitement level was high. The captains had agreed at the beginning not to choose the two best players of the seven who left the room, and all but the seven players knew this. When all of the others were chosen (five students) the captains offered to give the two boys to the opposite team because they were not good players. It was at this point that one of the "out" group boys said, "You're not choosing me on purpose." We then began our discussion into how the "out" group boys felt and how the "in" group members felt.

Both "out" group boys said they felt bad for not being chosen and one added that "I didn't really want to play anyway." "In" group members said it really felt good to be chosen. One person said she felt sad because "I like those two boys and wanted them on my team."

I then told the "out" group and the "in" group what we had done and that it had only been pretend in order for us to better understand how it feels to be left out.

Next I asked all of the boys to leave the room. The girls and I got ready for a discussion about the zoo. When the boys came back into the room we passed out pictures of our favorite animals in the zoo. I only called on the girls to relate their experiences at the zoo. The boys waved their hands to try to get my attention and interrupt the conversation. One boy said, "You never call on the boys!" I then asked the boys how it felt to be in the "out" group. Some of their comments were: "I got madder and madder!" "I got tired of holding my hand up and just gave up!" How did the girls feel? "I really liked it," said one girl. Another added, "Ladies first." The class laughed. We then discussed how people feel when they are "in" and "out." I asked, "Have you felt 'in' or 'out' in other situations?" Some responses were: "One time I had to stay in during recess and it felt bad." "Sometimes my older brother and sister get to do things that I don't get to do and it feels bad." "My daddy does special things with me on Saturdays and it really feels good." Their idea of "in" and "out" was based on personal likes and dislikes.

Our experience with the "ins" and "outs" lesson plan stimulated us to extend our unit of study to include two new concepts, preferential treatment and stereotypes.

LESSON 25   PREFERENTIAL TREATMENT

Objectives: As a result of this lesson, students should be able to:

    (1) develop a working definition of *stereotype*, such as "What you think a person is like just from seeing him or her or hearing what group he or she belongs to";

(2) define or cite examples of *preferential treatment*;

(3) describe the feelings frequently experienced by people who enjoy preferential treatment (pleasure, a desire to retain preferred status, a psychological distance from those not accorded such treatment, guilt at times) and by those who do not (anger, puzzlement, loneliness, rejection, desire to build own thing); and

(4) state advantages and disadvantages of classification systems.

Methods and Materials:

1. Divide the class into two groups according to some characteristic, such as those who wear glasses versus those who do not. Tell the students the basis for the division, and move those with one characteristic, like those who wear glasses, to the desks on the right side of the room and the rest to the left side of the room. Do not tell them how this division will be used.

2. Distribute ditto sheets on poetry or math puzzles to each group. The sheets with legible writing should be given to the students with glasses and the sheets given to the other students should be almost illegible.

3. Explain the sheet assignment to the entire class, but accept questions from and give explanations to only the group with glasses. If the students without glasses ask questions or complain about the illegible sheets, tell them: "Just do your work. Get busy and stop complaining." If pupils wearing glasses ask questions, give them clear, pleasant answers.

4. As the students begin work, circulate among the students wearing glasses, helping them complete their work. Ignore the no-glasses students, except to discipline them for talking or being unruly.

5. Since the students wearing glasses will finish first, give them five or ten minutes to chat and have a good time. If a no-glasses student finishes early, tell him to check over his answers or give him more work.

6. Following the brief recess of the students wearing glasses, conduct a general class discussion about what happened, how students felt, and why. Have a student volunteer write the opinions on the chalkboard under the categories "ins" and "outs."

7. Discuss what stereotype means. If no one knows, give a simple definition and ask students for some examples of stereotypes. Explain that some of them received preferential treatment for a physical characteristic, wearing glasses. Ask for other examples of stereotypes and how they are used in the school and in communities outside the school.

8. Discuss how classification systems have some advantages and some disadvantages.

Evaluation: Ask for student reactions to the following true incident and see if students use their new learnings. "A fight between a man and his wife took place late one night outside an apartment complex and the man smashed a car windshield with his fist in anger. An older woman woke up because of the noise and observed the incident, after which she called the police. When they arrived, they asked the woman, 'Was the man black or white?'"

A sixth grade teacher used the previous lesson plan and divided her class into a long-sleeved group (13 people) and a short-sleeved group (12 people). The short-sleeved group were the "ins" and the long-sleeved group were the "outs." The teacher described what happened:

Each student had a worksheet dealing with several reading skills, the only difference being legibility. The long sleeves' sheet was poorly hand-written, the short sleeves' sheet was printed and readable. Items were: (1) List ten words with short medial vowels; (2) List nine words that follow the vowel digraph rule; (3) Divide the following words into syllables: picture, watching, frankly, filler, and especially; (4) What are synonyms?; (5) What are antonyms?; and (6) Place these words in the correct alphabetical order: sing, science, sure, stop, staring, string, sang, sit.

This is what happened in my class. The long-sleeved group ("outs") responded:

1. We had sloppily written papers.
2. You let everyone else get up.
3. You made like you were for the short sleeves and against the long sleeves.
4. You let the short sleeves do whatever they wanted.
5. Are these scores going in the grade book? They shouldn't 'cause you helped them and not us!

The short-sleeved group ("ins") responded:

1. If we raised our hands, you helped us more than them guys.
2. We got all the privileges.
3. You were always mad at the long-sleeved group. They got what they deserved.
4. I felt sorry for them.

It was interesting for me to note that the long-sleeved "outs" had much more to say than the short-sleeved "ins." Some of the short-sleeved group didn't notice anything wrong at the time.

We continued our discussion for some time and gave examples from our lives outside of school in which we felt "in" and "out." Students then listed the advantages and disadvantages of classification systems:

Advantages   1. Help give a quick idea of what a person might be like.

2. Help describe people and sort them for computers.

3. Might predict a person's reactions to different situations.

Disadvantages 1. You judge people before you know them.

2. You focus on bad points people might have.

3. You don't really try to get to know what a person is really like.

There was considerable discussion about the evaluation case study, with advantages and disadvantages of sorting people given.

Loyalty to one's community is a condition for membership in that community. There are many current events that test this loyalty as evidenced in the following lesson plan.

LESSON 26   LOYALTY TO COMMUNITY

Objectives: As a result of this lesson, students should be able to:

(1) define the concept "community";

(2) observe that people feel loyal to their community in the face of some outside pressure or common disaster; and

(3) recognize that some form of cooperation may be necessary to solve a common community problem.

Methods and Materials:

1. Have students pretend that they are all members of a suburban neighborhood who live in beautiful homes with well kept yards. Most of them associate little with those outside the neighborhood.

2. They have just been informed that the freeway will cut through their neighborhood making the street in front of their homes a main thoroughfare. Up until now the only traffic on the street has been from residents and their friends. Now the heavy traffic will make the neighborhood noisy and dangerous for child play.

3. How will they react to the proposed freeway? Consider the possible effects of individual versus community action.

4. Two families immediately put their homes up for sale. How should the rest of you react to them?

5. Two other families seem reluctant to join the community in its efforts to influence city hall. How will the rest of you react to them?

6. Role play the situation and ask the following questions as well as others that come to mind:

   a. How did you feel when you first learned that the freeway was going through your neighborhood?

   b. How did it affect your relationship with your neighborhood acquaintances and friends?

   c. What role did cooperation play in your efforts? What role did competition play in your efforts?

   d. Did you feel that some people were being disloyal to the community? How did you feel about this and what did you do about it?

Evaluation: Observe student responses. Have a guest from the planning division of city hall come and discuss how situations like the one in this lesson do occur and what the most effective ways of relating to such situations are. See if students apply their new learnings in the interview situation.

Fortunately or unfortunately, it seems to be the case that many people need to experience intolerance and a lack of acceptance before they fully understand that they have been favored members of "in" groups in the school, by virtue of their relationships with teachers, other adults, and their peers. Children who have participated in the following three lesson plans have usually gained the insight that they need to build communities that have a good deal of tolerance and respect for people's differences.

LESSON 27   INTOLERANCE

Objectives: As a result of this lesson, students should be able to:

(1) define *intolerance;*

(2) relate some of the things that people can be intolerant of; and

(3) relate at least one harmful effect of intolerance.

Methods and Materials:

1. Along tables on one side of the room lay from seven to ten piles of paper. Each pile should have the same number of sheets as there are students in the room. The piles should be in a row with a stapler at each end. If possible the piles should be from one to two feet apart.

2. Divide the room in half. One-half believes that the only way to pick up the papers and staple them into a book is to go from left to right down the row. This is because it is the only right way to pick up papers, this is the way people read and therefore the only natural way, etc. The other half believes that the only right way to pick up papers and staple them is to go right to left down the row. This is because any other way is stupid and because most people are right handed and therefore it is more efficient.

3. Neither group is going to give up its ideas. If you believe you are right and all else are wrong you have to stick by your beliefs no matter what. Make sure this direction is clear to each group.

4. The whole class goes to pick up and staple their papers at the same time, each group starting at its end and going down the line.

5. Discuss what happened. Each group should give its reactions. Definitions of "intolerance" should be given. What happens when groups are intolerant of others should be discussed with references to communities outside the school. (Many examples exist in daily newspapers and other media.)

Evaluation: Note student responses during the activity. Read a case study of intolerance, perhaps from a book excerpt about Nazi Germany's banning of books, etc., and see if students can apply what they have learned to this situation.

LESSON 28   A FEAR OF DIFFERENCES

Objectives: As a result of this lesson, students should be able to:

(1) give a working definition of *intolerance;* and

(2) identify several examples of intolerance as it has affected persons in the past and today.

Methods and Materials:

1. Have the class form two equal groups and role play the following situation:

Two tribes live next to each other in the land of Ub. One is a tribe of sun god worshippers and the other is a tribe of tree spirit worshippers. The tribes have contact with each other through trade. Each tribe feels that they are worshipping the only true god and that the other tribe worships a false god and has strange and, therefore, barbaric customs. For the past year there has been a severe drought which has ruined crops and made hunting for food more difficult.

The sun god worshipper priests have told their people that the drought is a punishment because the tribe has been neglecting the sun god. The tribe has a special sun stone through which they worship the sun god. The priests say that in order to appease the sun god and end the drought the tribe must build a temple to place the sun stone in. The temple must face west and it must be located in such a way that when the sun sets on March 22 and on September 21 the sun's rays will touch the stone at a special angle. The priests have determined the right angle. They have found a place on a nearby hill for the temple. There are other places but this is the best place as far as convenience is concerned. The only obstacle is a large tree that would stand in the way of the sun's rays. If it could be cut down the temple could be easily built. It is necessary to build the temple quickly so that it is finished before September 21 and so that the drought will be ended and the tribal crops saved. The village depends mostly on crops for its living and the crops need rain to grow.

The tree spirit worshipper priests have told their people that the drought is a punishment because the tribe has been neglecting the spirits of the trees. The tribe worships spirits. These spirits help the tribe by helping the hunters find game. The tribe depends mainly on hunting for its survival. It is the duty of the tribe to find homes for the tree spirits. This is done by consecrating trees that are especially large and with many limbs. The priests have said that the drought is being caused by the tree spirit Ni who is mad because his tree is dying and the tribe has not found a new one for him. Tree consecration takes a month and is a long, involved ceremony. It takes time to find the right tree, but the priests have found one. It is on the same nearby hill where the sun god worshippers want to build their temple. The tree is the one they want to cut down.

Both tribes meet on the hill. Five men are selected from each tribe to discuss the situation with each other to decide what to do. Then they will meet with the other tribe. The selected men are:

Sun-Worshippers:

   High Priest. He believes that their god wants the temple where they are going to place it. Furthermore he believes the other tribe to be heathens. He would like to convert them to his religion. He feels a good first step would be to destroy their gods and he sees a good way to do this is to cut down that tree, even if it means war.

Tribal Leader. He is worried by the drought. If it continues much longer he is afraid that the village may die off. He is anxious to please the gods. He also feels that the other tribe is taking up land for hunting that could be put to much better use as cropland. He would welcome a war as a way to show those heathens who has the true god and to obtain a bit more land.

Farmer. He has been hurt by the drought and will do anything to appease the sun god. If a temple will stop the drought then he will insist that the temple be built. However, he does not want war. If there was a war he and his sons would have to go to help fight and then no one would be there to take care of his farm and plant the crops. Then again, if the drought continues he would lose his land anyway.

Merchant. He does not want war, it would hurt his trade with the tree spirit worshipper tribe. He would like to avoid all the trouble and just find another location for the temple.

Old Man. He knows from experience that wars are not always the best way to solve problems. He feels the other tribe has barbaric customs and feels his tribe would be better off with little contact with their strange ways. He has seen droughts come and go before in his long life and is not particularly worried by this one.

Tree-Spirit Worshippers:

High Priest. He looked a long time before he found this tree. It is the best tree for Ni in the area. He feels nothing but contempt for the sun worshippers and their false god. He does not want their temple so close to his village. He is worried that some of the heathenish customs of the sun worshippers may be picked up by the young people in his tribe. A war to defeat the sun worshippers would stop this once and for all.

Tribal Leader. The drought has driven much of the game away. He is anxious to appease Ni and get the affairs of the village back to normal. If the drought continues much longer, much of the tribe will starve. He feels that the farmers of the other tribe are taking some of the tribe's land and scaring the game away. He feels a successful war would stop this encroachment.

Hunter. Hunting has been hard. His family is hungry. He wants to quickly please Ni and find a home for him. He feels the tribe could win a war but he is afraid that by the time everything got settled after a war many people would have starved.

Trader. He makes his living by supplying the village with many of the things they can't make. A war would ruin his trade and his living for quite a while—no matter who won. He feels one tree is as good as another.

Wise Man. He feels that Ni might be appeased into taking a lesser tree. He does not see why it has to be this one particular tree. He feels, however, that the barbaric sun worshippers should be taught a lesson. He is worried by their strange ways and their worship of an alien god.

Each group should decide which students will role play the five men.

2. Following role playing of the incident, tolerance and intolerance that emerged from this situation should be discussed. Also, tolerance and intolerance in students' lives should be discussed.

Evaluation: Please note student responses and bring contemporary news story to class for discussion.

LESSON 29   GAINING ACCEPTANCE IN A NEW COMMUNITY

Objectives: As a result of this lesson, students should be able to:

(1) identify and discuss some problems of gaining acceptance facing immigrants to an area; and

(2) identify and discuss ways in which community members can issue positive invitations to others to join their community.

Methods and Materials:

1. Read or distribute copies of the background information on Nova Terra to the class and then have the class form into groups of at least six to play the roles specified in the game.

Twenty-five years ago a spaceship from Earth carrying 750 colonists crash landed on the planet they called Nova Terra. The spaceship was bound for another planet in another part of the galaxy. The equipment on board and the plants and animals carried were chosen because they would be useful for the conditions on the other planet; they were not planned for Nova Terra. When the ship crashed, it destroyed the communications system and the engines, making it impossible for the people on the ship either to get off the planet or to get help from anyone else. Many of the animals carried in the ship died on Nova Terra and most of the plants were not suitable. Like the Pilgrims in America back in the history of Earth many of the colonists died in the first hard years of learning what plants would grow and of learning what they could eat that already grew on the planet. The sudden storms that swept across the planet took many lives until the people learned how to forecast the weather. Gradually the colonists have been able to build up their farms and their homes and the colony is successfully growing. The colonists have explored the planet and have discovered that most of the planet is water with one large continent the colonists called Terra Firma and one small island called Parva.

Now the council of the colony is meeting to consider a new crisis that is facing the colony. The council is made of five people (chaplain, successful farmer, young farmer, doctor, teacher), each one representing one hundred of the present colonists. Yesterday another ship in distress landed. It is carrying 450 colonists from the settlement on Mars outbound to another planet. Although the grandparents of these people from Mars had come from Earth in the first place, the time that their families had lived on Mars had changed their language somewhat and changed their customs from those on Earth. Now the captain from the spaceship is appealing to the council for permission for the Martian colonists to settle here on Nova Terra. The communicators on the ship have been ruined, but it would be possible to fix the short range drive of the ship, but not the engines that could carry it across the galaxy. If the short range drive is fixed and the ship is able to lift off, the problem is that nothing is known of the area of the galaxy. No one on Nova Terra knows whether there is another planet close by that would be suitable for human life.

Thus the council faces three choices. They can insist that the spaceship be fixed and the colonists from Mars leave and take their chances on finding a suitable planet somewhere close. They can allow the colonists to stay on Nova Terra but insist that they settle on the small island of Parva instead of joining with the settlement on the large continent of Terra Firma. The council must listen to the request of the captain of the spaceship and then discuss the question of what to do with these people. Then they must vote with three of the five agreeing on the same course of action.

The roles to be played are:

Captain. The captain of the spaceship from Mars. He pleads for his people to be allowed full participation in the settlement on Terra Firma. He feels that their chances of finding another planet they could survive on are very small and that there is not enough room on the island of Parva to allow the colonists to live comfortably.

Chaplain. He feels that all of the people must be allowed to stay as part of the settlement on Terra Firma. He thinks all people are part of his responsibility to God.

Successful Farmer. He is opposed to allowing the people to stay at all. He feels that they suffered so much in their first years that others can too. He has several children and wants to leave them a large farm and a bright future. He also thinks that if they allow the Martians to remain the settlement will be overcrowded soon. He does not want his children or grandchildren to have to make the long, dangerous space voyage to find another planet because this one becomes overcrowded. He also does not want to allow them to stay on Parva because he does not think that they will be satisfied there and will try to take over Terra Firma.

Young Farmer. He would like the new colonists to be allowed to stay. He was only a baby when their own ship landed and does not really remember the time of suffering. What he does know is that he is tired of the same small group of people, and he would like to see new people and new things.

Doctor. He would like to forbid the people from staying. He is afraid that they will bring new diseases with them and that the people from his own settlement will get sick because they are not used to the diseases.

Teacher. He would prefer them to stay, but only on the island of Parva. He thinks that the settlement on Nova Terra needs new ideas since it has been cut off from the rest of the galaxy for so long, but he is afraid that the people from Mars have ways of behaving that would be bad for the people of Nova Terra, so they should be kept to themselves to see what they are like.

2. After the students in each group have discussed the issues and had time to vote, break for a discussion to find out what each group decided. Discuss what people thought they would lose or gain by admitting new people and how the new colonists felt about the situation. Also, discuss similar situations in American history.

Evaluation: Observe student responses to class activities. Ask students to bring to class the following day examples from the newspaper of events that demonstrate what they learned today.

LESSON 30   JAMES GOES TO SCHOOL

Objectives: As a result of this lesson, students should be able to:

(1) define "mainstreaming" as merging special education students into regular classrooms;

(2) recognize the special needs of each person; and

(3) identify ways to meet such needs.

Methods and Materials:

1. Read the following story to the children:

   James is a good-looking boy. He has curly black hair and a big bright smile. James got a red wagon for Christmas and he loves pulling his friends in his wagon. James often plays with children who are younger than he is because the children his age are all in school. James wishes he could go to school. He's almost six but his mother won't let him go. She worries about James because he is deaf. He can't hear like most children. He laughs and cries just like other children and has all of the same feelings. James can write his name, tie his shoes, and button his shirt ... and he wants to come to school.

2. Ask the children, "Do you think James should be allowed to come to school? Give reasons for your answer." "How might we learn from James and how might he learn from us?" "What special help will James need and do we have the special help to give him?" "Are there special education teachers who can help James become part of the regular classroom?" Define "becoming part of the regular classroom" as "mainstreaming."

3. Continue the story:

   One day, Mrs. Parker, the kindergarten teacher, talks to James's mother. She tells his mother that she would like to have James in class. Mrs. Parker says that James's mother can bring him at any time. James's mother agrees to bring James for a few weeks to see how things go.

4. The following questions may be useful for class discussion.

   a. What can the class do to get ready for James? (For example, the special education teacher might spend some time preparing the class.)

   b. What are some things James might need help with? Some things he won't need help with?

Evaluation: Have a person from a community agency come into the class, someone with expertise in working with the deaf. Observe what questions the children in class ask.

LESSON 31 CONFORMITY

Objectives: As a result of this lesson, students should be able to:

(1) discuss the view that a community can be described by what the members have in common;

(2) understand that when people adopt certain characteristics to be part of a group, they are conforming to that group (If a person doesn't conform he is usually asked to leave the group or community.);

(3) understand that some conformity is necessary for a community's survival; and

(4) understand that conformity can have negative connotations in situations where conformity conflicts with personal integrity.

Methods and Materials:

1. Select four or five volunteers to be part of a special No-Classroom-Cleanup group. All members in this group will have to do the homeroom cleanup work for that afternoon. To be members of this group the students will have to do two things: they will have to hold one of their arms in a sling position and they will have to start every sentence they say or write with the word "peacock."

2. Organize the classroom cleanup for that day. Explain that there is a special group that does not have to do the cleanup. Members of this group have things in common. Anyone who wants to may join this group, but all members of this group must follow the characteristics of the community. When a student feels he has determined the common characteristics, he may ask a member to see if he is right. If he is right and agrees to follow the group, he is then a member of the group.

3. When most students are in the No-Classroom-Cleanup community, announce that it is no longer necessary to hold arms in the sling position and say "peacock" to get out of doing cleanup work. There will be no cleanup today. Continue the free period a little longer and observe reactions. Actions should stop and the community should fall apart.

4. Ask students to analyze what happened in a class discussion and compare and contrast this experience to student and adult behavior in communities, for example with suitable dress patterns.

Evaluation: Ask students to write an essay on advantages and disadvantages of conformity.

One of the main goals for the study of community in elementary schools is to help children realize that they have political potency: they can make decisions that will make differences in their own lives and the lives of others in communities. One way to emphasize this matter is to study and participate in the formation of the classroom community. In the process, children can understand and discuss simple kindnesses, family rules, school rules, and political processes. A kindergarten teacher developed the following lesson plan to help her children understand the importance of simple kindnesses within a classroom community.

LESSON 32   SIMPLE KINDNESSES

Objectives: As a result of this lesson, students should be able to:

(1) identify and attach meanings to terms such as "please," "thank you," "you're welcome," and "excuse me"; and
(2) incorporate such terms when appropriate into their daily activities.

Methods and Materials:

1. Build a game board with a spinner and a turtle at the center of it. The turtle should have the terms in (1) above, plus others of your choice; each term will have its space on the turtle's back. The child will spin and then all the class will discuss how the term should be used and give examples of when it would be used and where.
   a. Example: If a child spins "thank you," I'll ask the class "When do we say 'thank you'?" and they'll reply something like "When someone gives you something." I would then pursue other instances such as "When someone says something nice to you such as, 'Suzie, that's a very pretty dress you have on today.'" Then I would ask the child who was the spinner to give an example of a real situation such as "I said thank you when Tommy gave me a cookie at lunch."

Evaluation: Observe student responses to see who participates and in what way. (Try to be sure all participate.) See if students begin to incorporate these phrases into their everyday activities with other students.

Early elementary teachers have found this game to be an excellent way to involve students in simple kindnesses. One teacher remarked, "I used to give little sermons all the time to try to get children to learn simple manners but the turtle game makes it easier and more fun for all of us." Children like the active participation that goes with the game and they seem to enjoy teaching each other without really knowing they are doing so. They like to name the turtle and when they think a student isn't mannerly they say, "Remember what Tommy Turtle says." The turtle game can be adjusted to teach other concepts also.

The following lesson plan focuses on toleration for differences in general and on a particular issue, relating to an adopted child who has been treated unkindly by another student.

LESSON 33   ADOPTION

Objectives: As a result of this lesson, students should be able to:

(1) examine the generalization that persons get along with each other better if they have a good deal of tolerance for differences; and

(2) suggest ways in which tolerance for differences might be acted out in their classroom and school.

Methods and Materials:

1. Read the following story to the children:

   Jack is in the sixth grade and will soon be twelve years old. He is an average student and well-liked by the other children.

   One morning on the playground before school Jack and another sixth grader become involved in a heated argument. Just as Jack seems to be winning the argument, the other boy suddenly shouts, "Well, at least I'm not adopted!" Without really thinking Jack replied, "Neither am I!" The other boy shouted back, "Oh yes you are. I heard your mom say that you were!"

   Jack hadn't heard this before and never suspected he was adopted. (Ask the children, "What do you think Jack was thinking at this time? How does he feel?")

   Jack spent the rest of the day deep in thought. His teacher noticed that he seemed inattentive and somewhat disturbed. Finally she asked Jack if anything was wrong. (What do you think Jack said? How did he feel about the teacher's question?)

   On the way home Jack thought about what the boy had said and what he would say to his parents. That night at supper Jack was unusually quiet. His parents asked what was wrong. (What do you think Jack said?)

Suddenly Jack told them what had happened on the playground at school. He demanded an answer as to whether what the boy said was true. Much to his amazement, his parents said it was true—that they had adopted him as a baby. (How do you think Jack felt? Do you think he should have been told by his parents before? If so, when should he have been told?) Jack's parents said they should have told him before and were planning on telling him. They all had a long talk and the parents explained that the important thing is that a child is loved and they truly loved Jack. (What do you think were some other things Jack and his parents talked about during this time?)

Evaluation: Observe student responses. Have a guest from an adoption agency and see what questions children ask.

An early elementary teacher used the following lesson plan with her children. It focuses on family rules.

LESSON 34   FAMILY RULES, RESPONSIBILITIES, AND OPPORTUNITIES

Objectives: As a result of this lesson, students should be able to:

(1) know the meaning of rules, responsibilities, and opportunities and see relationships between these terms;
(2) give reasons for rules and responsibilities;
(3) discuss reasons why rules change with age and situations; and
(4) suggest other rules a family might have and make choices as to rules they think their family should have.

Methods and Materials:

1. Read the following story: One night after supper, Betty and Steve were watching television with their big sister Ann. Mother was washing the dishes and Father was reading the newspaper.

   When Mother finished in the kitchen, she came into the living room and said, "Okay, Betty and Steve, it's time for bed."

   "Ah, gee, Mom! Why can't we stay up to see another program?" asked Betty.

2. Select five children to go to the front of the room. Have them role play to see what they would do in this situation.

3. Begin the discussion by asking, "Who decided what Betty and Steve should do? Who made the bedtime rules? Who should make bedtime rules? Why didn't Ann, the big sister, get sent to bed? How do you think Steve and Betty felt? Will you be treated differently at home when you are older? The same? Who should change rules at home? Are there special occasions, such as when grandparents visit or at Christmas, when rules are changed at home?"

4. Have the children group themselves with four to five children in each group. Ask each group to do a small skit on "situations when rules are changed."

4. Give each child a ditto sheet with three columns: column headings are rules, responsibilities, and opportunities. Have each child write appropriate comments in each column in order to describe rules, opportunities, and responsibilities in their homes. Discuss what children wrote in class.

Evaluation: Observe children in role playing and skits. Ask the children to take their ditto sheets home, discuss them with others in their homes, and add to them for next day's discussion.

Children experience the need to make and maintain their own rules in a variety of settings outside the classroom and school. These experiences can provide the teacher with subject matter for active learning in the classroom. The next lesson plan demonstrates this matter.

LESSON 35   BUILDING A GO-KART

Objective: As a result of this lesson, students should be able to:

(1) analyze and take a stand on the idea that rule making is necessary whenever two or more people get together and can be a cooperative endeavor.

Methods and Materials:

1. Read the following case study or story and have students role play each of the roles in front of the class:

Mike, who is five years old, will begin kindergarten this year. His brother is eight and his sister is one year old. Sometimes Mike gets along with his brother just fine. At other times they fight. Mike has a red wagon that is about three years old. He uses it to ride down the slightly sloping driveway in his court and also to carry toys, sand, and other things. One day Mike's brother and his friend got an idea: "Let's build a go-kart like the older boys use in the 'Junior 500'!" (Mike and his brother saw the "Junior 500" the day before.) Then Mike's brother said, "Can we take your wagon apart and use the wheels for the go-kart?"

(After the role player responds, have the class react to the question.) Mike decided to let his brother take his wagon apart and use the wheels, but he wondered if they should ask his father or mother before taking the wagon apart.

(After the role player responds, have the class react to the question.) The wheels are now connected to the bottom board of the go-kart, but the boys run out of lumber and nails. One of the boys said, "Let's go over to the new houses they're building and get some boards and nails."

(Ask the boys if they should pick up the lumber they think the workmen don't need and use the lumber and any nails they find for the go-kart or if the men are working at the house should they ask them for the lumber and nails? After the role players respond, have the class react.) The go-kart is now finished and the boys paint it red and put old carpeting on the seat. One boy said, "Let's make some rules for using the go-kart."

(Ask the other boy, who is the role player if he thinks rules should be made and if so what they should be. Then ask the class to enter into the discussion.)

Mike, his brother, and his brother's friend are now ready to try out the go-kart in their driveway.

(Ask the three role players who should ride in the go-kart first. Then get the class reaction.)

Mike's friend, who has been on vacation, wants to ride in the go-kart even though he didn't help build it.

(Ask the role players and then the class to react to this request.)

The next day, Mike has a fight with his brother and his brother and brother's friend say, "It isn't your go-kart anyway 'cause you didn't build it."

(Ask the person playing Mike's role to react after which the class should suggest a response.)

Mike's brother's friend has a sister who is eleven years old and she wants to ride the go-kart.

(What should the boys say? is the question to ask the role players and class.)

Mike's brother and his friend use the go-kart most of the time because

they can handle it easier than Mike can. Mike says to himself, "I wish I had my wagon back 'cause it's more for boys my age anyway than a go-kart."
(Discuss this comment with the role players and class.)

Evaluation: Observe student responses throughout the lesson.

A teacher who planned this lesson and tried it out with her early elementary children describes her experience:

I probably learned more than the children with this exciting lesson based on what really happened to a child in my class. At first I had a lot of scattered ideas as to how to teach the lesson and the lesson itself didn't jell until the end due to two erroneous assumptions I made:

1. that the children were not going to respond to the questions readily; and
2. that we wouldn't have enough material to fill up the half hour I wanted to spend on it.

One thing I did to liven up the story was to bring in a picture-drawing of a child in a go-kart. The children really liked that.

One thing that I really emphasized in the lesson was the importance of sharing at home and at school. At the end of the lesson I asked one of the students to throw a ball to another student in front of the class but not throw it to a third student who wanted to join them. Then I asked the student who was left out how it felt. Finally I had the other students in the role playing experience being left out of the ball tossing and they too said that it really felt bad. This prompted a discussion of other incidents where students shared or didn't share.

The following lesson plan on school rules, responsibilities, and opportunities complements the previous lesson plan.

LESSON 36   SCHOOL RULES, RESPONSIBILITIES, AND OPPORTUNITIES

Objectives: As a result of this lesson, students should be able to:

(1) know the meaning of rules, responsibilities, and opportunities and see relationships between these terms;

(2) give reasons for rules and responsibilities;

(3) discuss reasons why rules change; and

(4) weigh their role in changing rules.

Methods and Materials:

1. Have an open-ended discussion on rules in school in order to "brainstorm" a number of ideas and feelings. Then list on the board rules the school has, responsibilities these rules entail, and opportunities that come from such rules and responsibilities. For example, there is a school rule that says *No running in the halls*. This rule makes me responsible for not running in the halls and sometimes asking others in a nice way not to run in the halls. In turn I then have the opportunity to go safely from one part of the building to another part of the building.

2. Divide the class into groups with five children in each group. Ask each group to act out what school would be like without rules. (You will obviously have to keep them within certain bounds.) Discuss what a "school without rules" would be like. Once again, discuss responsibilities and opportunities that follow from rules.

3. Ask each student to name his or her most valuable possessions. Discuss what rules and laws protect such possessions. Have each student name a friend not in the classroom. Discuss what rules and laws protect this person. Be sure, once again, to discuss opportunities that flow from such rules so that children don't see rules as simply protecting them.

4. Have each student write a one sentence rule that would make school or home a better place to live. Ask the students to explain why they think the rule is necessary.

5. Ask students if all rules need to be written down. This should stimulate a good discussion in class.

Evaluation: Observe student responses. Bring in copies of rules from different settings. Discuss how some rules still in writing (such as *No loitering in grocery stores*) are no longer used. Discuss.

It is important that children see rules as changeable. It is equally important to have them understand that they have the political potency to influence how rules will be changed. The next lesson plan was constructed to involve students in political processes in order to realize their political potency.

LESSON 37   POLITICAL PROCESSES

Objectives: As a result of this lesson, students should be able to:

(1) communicate their beliefs to other students in general and to a leader of their choice in particular;

(2) identify and define three sources of power (expertise, charisma, and emotional support); and

(3) discuss the role of trade-offs and compromises in the political process.

Methods and Materials:

1. Tell the class that they should imagine that when their class graduates from elementary school they will have saved a total of $400 by selling baked goods, having car washes, and the like. Inform them that there will be 100 students in the graduating class.

2. Divide the class into four groups and have each group choose a representative. Tell the students in each group that they must unanimously agree on how the money should be spent, although the entire amount of money doesn't have to go for one thing.

3. Inform the students that they can talk to their representatives at any time during the "debate" but they can't talk to members of other groups.

4. Place the four representatives in a small circle in the middle of the room with their constituents behind them and begin the debate over how the money should be spent with the stipulation that the four must agree on a method of deciding how the money should be spent. (They may decide, for example, on simple majority rule or they may insist on unanimous agreement.)

5. Take the four representatives out of the room so that they can talk privately without pressure from their constituents. Explain to constituents that state and federal representatives also have geographical distance from their constituents. (Note how constituents react to their representatives when they return to the room.)

6. Resume debate and have representatives come to a conclusion.

7. Discuss how students felt about what they experienced.

8. Explain that constituents didn't have a position of authority as a source of power as did the representative but instead they could rely on expertise (such as the ability to verbalize), charisma, and emotional support.

Evaluation: Observe student responses. Discuss one or more television shows where characters use different sources of power. Note how characters have to compromise and use trade-offs in order to get what they want. Ask students to write brief stories concerning how they have been involved in activities in which they used their political power.

The lesson plan on political processes has been one of our most successful plans because students are actively involved in trying to get what they want and in the process use all kinds of devices to try to influence their peers. One of the groups usually wants to buy something nice for the principal and teachers, such as a trophy or a tree for the front of the school. Another group usually wants to give the money to various charities. Most groups, however, want to use the money to go to an amusement park or some other similar place. This diversity of responses leads to lively discussion concerning using our resources for ourselves versus using such resources for others. And one student added to the discussion by saying, "Even if you want to give the money to a charity or an ecology tree you are doing it because it makes you feel good and isn't that being selfish?"

Constituents who are left in the room after their representatives leave the room are very nervous about "being sold out." When their representatives return to the room, the constituents quiz them to be sure their interests are being represented. And all students recognize that some compromise and many trade-offs are part of the political process.

A key concept in understanding conflict within and between communities is multiple causation. When we become emotional about an issue, we tend to only see one cause and our rhetoric represents this view. It is also important for students to understand that each person has a different perception of an event and sets his or her own value priorities according to this perception. The following lesson plan relates to these issues.

LESSON 38   LANDLORD-TENANT CONFRONTATION

Objectives: As a result of this lesson, students should consider the idea that:

(1) a given action or event has many causes;

(2) people concerned with an event interpret what occurs according to their own priority of values (belief systems);

(3) people who wish to influence the outcome of an event behave on the basis of their own priority of values; and

(4) landlords commonly have a different priority of values than do tenants.

Methods and Materials:

1. Announce to the class that a landlord has just asked his financially poor tenant's family to leave their apartment. The task is to identify reasons why this confrontation has occurred. Tell them that two students can act out the meeting between the landlord and tenant, and by viewing this scene the class may be able to estimate why this event happened.

2. Select one volunteer to play the role of landlord. Hand him a card labeled LANDLORD citing some reasons why he is evicting the tenants. Tell him that he should add other reasons as well.

3. Select another volunteer to play the role of tenant. Hand him a card labeled TENANT citing some reasons he has not paid the rent. He can also think of other reasons.

4. Before the role playing begins, suggest that each student mentally or actually divide a sheet of paper into two columns, one titled LANDLORD and the other TENANT. As the scene is acted out, they are to record the reasons for the actions of the two characters.

5. Have the two actors come before the class and describe the setting somewhat in this fashion: "We'll imagine that the landlord has just knocked on the door of the tenant's apartment. When the tenant opens it, the landlord steps in and says that the family will have to move. When the tenant asks why, the landlord starts to give his reasons. Then the tenant answers back. Now, let's begin with the landlord knocking on the door."

6. When the sociodrama has gone far enough to elicit a variety of reasons or arguments on both sides, ask the two characters to switch roles and play the scene again.

7. After the second playing of the scene, conduct a discussion of the event focusing on individual viewpoints, values, and feelings in regard to the event, its causes, and its solution.

8. You may wish to add to this lesson by introducing the matter of vocations: A minister calls on the tenant who is a member of his or her congregation and an attorney joins the landlord in the confrontation. Students can then discuss how the "minister" and "attorney" played their roles.

Evaluation: Observe student responses. Using a controversial event from the newspaper, hold another discussion on why the event may have occurred. More than one cause should be proposed. Or come to class the next day all excited about a controversial event and give one cause for the event. See if any students disagree and in the process argue for multiple causation.

SUGGESTED ACTIVITIES

The landlord-tenant lesson has stimulated a good deal of discussion in elementary school classes. Students quickly learn the meaning of multiple causation by taking the concept apart and examining each part. In using the game we were somewhat surprised at how many students have had some kind of experience with landlords. They draw from this experience in discussing the lesson. A number of follow-up activities may be used.

1. Have a landlord and a tenant as guests in the class. The thought that goes into preparing interview questions can be most useful to observe.
2. Have one or more students interview landlords and tenants with cassette recorders after which the recordings are played back to the class for further discussion.
3. Have students write congressmen for information on legislation concerning landlord-tenant relations, legislation passed or in process.
4. Examine copies of leases in class and discuss them.
5. Check on legal services available to landlords and tenants and perhaps have an attorney as a class guest.
6. Take a field trip to city hall and talk to city planners about relations between landlords and tenants. Note that the city itself is a landlord for many tenants.
7. Get information about road building that gives quick access around rather than through the city. Discuss how this influences housing patterns and therefore landlord-tenant relations.
8. Get information on how rezoning takes place in the area, particularly from residential to commercial. Note how this influences housing patterns and therefore landlord-tenant relations. Also note how this influences schools.
9. Get information about inward and outward migration to and from the city. Give particular attention to the "flight to the suburbs" and how this influences housing patterns, churches, and businesses. A tour of a city area and a suburban area may be helpful with respect to this topic.
10. Design an ideal city. Build a model of this city. Describe landlord-tenant relations in this city.

The final topic included in our discussion of the need for community is relating to friends. Each of us knows the importance of having a few very close friends in a community, people who can be counted on for support. Elementary school children find the discussion of the importance of friends of special interest.

LESSON 39   RELATING TO FRIENDS

Objectives: As a result of this lesson, students should be able to:

(1) define what is meant by "a friend";
(2) communicate to others in the class how it feels to have a close friend; and
(3) how it feels to be in a situation where you don't have a friend.

Methods and Materials:

1. Begin the following story: Tommy is a six year old who was coming to school for the first time. Tommy arrived at school and saw a little girl go in with her big brother and a little boy go in with his mother. Tommy felt very lonesome and wanted to leave.
2. Then ask, "What should Tommy do?" (Some possible answers are to run down the street and go home, go into the school with the others, and sit down and cry.)
3. Continue the story: Tommy decided he didn't want to go to school because he was afraid. He started down the street crying. All of a sudden he bumped into something. He looked up and saw a very jolly face staring at him.
4. Ask, "Should Tommy say 'excuse me' or should he just walk down the street, or should he do something else?"
5. Continue the story: Tommy said 'excuse me' and the jolly face asked him what his name was. Then the man said, "I'm Mr. Perry and I own the grocery store near the school and you should be in school."
6. Ask, "What should Tommy say to Mr. Perry or what should Tommy do?"
7. Continue the story: Tommy knew he should be in school and so he walked back to school. A friendly teacher put her arm around Tommy and told him to come in.
8. Ask, "How do you think Tommy felt now?"
9. Continue the story: The teacher showed Tommy to a desk and gave him a box of crayons with his name on it.
10. Ask, "How do you think Tommy felt after this?"
11. Continue the story: It was soon playtime in the room and Tommy was the only one who didn't go to an interest center but instead sat at his

desk. Joe and Ted came over and asked him to build a house with them in the block corner.

12. Ask, "How did Tommy feel before the boys invited him to the block corner and how did he feel when he was asked to the block corner?"
13. Ask some of the following as follow-up questions:
    a. Have you felt like Tommy at times? Explain.
    b. How can we invite other children to be part of activities so they don't feel lonely?

Evaluation: Observe student actions and responses. Ask them to draw two pictures: one of them with a friend and one feeling lonely without a friend.

All children experience some fear when they are in new situations and away from the security of normal friendships. Going to camp is such an experience.

LESSON 40   NEW FRIENDS AT CAMP

Objectives: As a result of this lesson, students should be able to:

(1) list the characteristics of friendship;
(2) communicate the feelings associated with being in a new situation without friends; and
(3) communicate the feelings associated with new friendships in new situations.

Methods and Materials:

1. Begin telling the following story: This was seven-year-old Becky's first summer at camp. She was afraid of being alone when her parents left. Her counselor was nice to her so she didn't cry. Inside her cabin Becky met seven girls. One girl named Jane was crying.
2. Ask, "What should Becky do?" (Some responses may be "Ignore the girl" or "Talk to her.")
3. Continue the story: After Jane stopped crying and felt better, Becky met Susan who was very friendly. Marie, however, did not talk at all but did smile at Becky.
4. Ask, "How could the girls get to know each other better?"
5. Continue the story: The girls went to the lodge for lunch. They had beans but Becky didn't like beans.

6. Ask, "What should Becky do?" (Options include eat them anyway, don't eat them but say nothing, don't eat them and tell others at the table.)
7. Continue the story: After lunch Becky went to the handicraft shop and made a pretty bracelet. Then she went to the archery range with her new friends and shot arrows from a bow. Before going to sleep at night the girls and their counselor sat around and told what they liked best about the day.
8. Ask, "What do you think Becky said?"

Evaluation: Observe student responses. Ask students to draw a picture of a time when they were in a new situation and made a new friend.

One of the most difficult issues related to friendship according to elementary students we've talked to is "telling on a friend" when the friend has done something wrong. The following lesson plan relates to this issue.

LESSON 41   TELLING ON A FRIEND

Objectives: As a result of this lesson, students should be able to:
(1) define characteristics of a friendship;
(2) relate the feelings associated with the conflict between loyalty to the community as a whole versus loyalty to a friend who has done something wrong; and
(3) relate incidents similar to the one in the story.

Methods and Materials:

1. Read the following story to the class: While the class was standing outside getting ready for lunch, your best friend asked the teacher for permission to go back to the room to get something. The teacher said, "Yes," and your best friend ran toward the room.

You remembered something you forgot and asked permission to get it from the room and received such permission. Just as you opened the door you saw your friend take something out of Jim's desk and hurriedly close the desk.

After lunch the teacher said, "Fifty cents is missing from Jim's desk. Do any of you know anything about it?

2. Ask, "What would you do in this situation if you saw your friend do this?"

3. Discuss students' answers.

Evaluation: Observe student responses. Ask students for incidents like the one in the story and discuss such incidents.

One class of students, intrigued by the dilemma of loyalty to friend versus loyalty to the community, answered as follows:

JEAN: I would tell even if she was my best friend because you know it's just not right to steal.

ANNA: I wouldn't tell. I'd tell my friend to put it back.

JANE: I wouldn't want to tell because if someone told on me I wouldn't feel too good so I'd tell him to put it back and if he wouldn't I'd tell the teacher. But if someone told on me I'd feel guilt and be mad at my friend. What kind of friend would "squeal" on you anyway?

JOE: I wouldn't tell because we don't know that it was money that my friend took out of Jim's desk. Maybe he was just getting his magic marker back or something.

TEACHER: What if the friend was a big bully?

GEORGE: I'd tell the teacher but I wouldn't tell her in front of the big bully. He might beat me up.

JOE: I wouldn't get beat up. I wouldn't tell on the big bully for sure.

TEACHER: Would the amount of money make any difference? What if two dollars were stolen?

JOE: I'd tell then. If it was the bully, though, I'd probably send you a note so I wouldn't get found out and get beat up.

MARION: Tell the teacher and have her search the thief.

JOE: Would that be legal?

The school community can be greatly enhanced by involving people of all ages in its activities. In recent years, retired persons have been active in some elementary schools in a variety of roles: they have helped staff tutoring programs and they have introduced crafts or hobbies and their previous vocations to the children.[8] The two lesson plans that follow relate to the issue of adult-child covenants.

LESSON 42 A RETIRED FRIEND

Objectives: As a result of this lesson, students should be able to:

    (1) identify some of the problems and opportunities associated with the life of a retired person in our society; and

    (2) recognize the important role that all persons regardless of age can play in the school and neighborhood community.

Methods and Materials:

1. Read or have a student read the following story:

    Brad had a very special friend, Mr. Lewis, who lived next door. Mr. Lewis, a retired citizen, lived alone for his wife had died several years ago. His two daughters had married some time ago and moved into the city. Mr. Lewis was often lonely without his wife or daughters. Some days after school Brad would visit Mr. Lewis and help him with his greenhouse plants. On occasion Mr. Lewis would take Brad to town, after getting his parents' permission, to stop at the ice cream shop for a treat. They rode in Mr. Lewis's old truck, which was fun. One day Brad thought to himself, "I wonder if Mr. Lewis might like to visit our classroom at school."

2. The following questions might help guide the class in its discussion of the story:

    a. What might Mr. Lewis do as a guest in the classroom? (If students mention bringing in some plants, talking about them, and perhaps helping them get some seeds started you might suggest a field trip to Mr. Lewis's greenhouse?) Then ask, "What might we do and see at the greenhouse?"

    b. How might we invite Mr. Lewis to come to our classroom? Should we consider possible questions to ask him ahead of time?

    c. One of the students might suggest that Mr. Lewis talk about how times have remained the same and changed since he was our age in school. This would be interesting to discuss.

    d. What might we do to follow up on the visit of Mr. Lewis?

Evaluation: Have children look through magazines for pictures of retired people and discuss their lives.

                Have the children write stories about retired people they know and read them to people in a nursing home.

LESSON 43 TODAY AND YESTERDAY

Objectives: As a result of this lesson, students should be able to:

(1) discuss similarities and differences between people of different ages;

(2) involve themselves in conducting interviews with people of different ages; and

(3) list several differences in life today compared to life in the past.

Methods and Materials:

1. Collect and bring to class a variety of resource books, magazines, paste, shoe boxes, scissors, and note cards.

2. Talk with students about their daily life at school and home with special emphasis on food, transportation, and recreation. (Add other topics if you wish.) Read about and discuss concepts of how people in times past lived and compare and contrast daily life today with daily life in the past.

3. Instruct each student to develop at least three questions they would like to ask someone ten or so years older and someone thirty to fifty years older. Ask students to print these questions on index cards.

4. Collect all the cards and place them in a big box. Students can assist in making the box by looking for pictures of people of all ages in the magazines. These people will be involved in different activities. Paste these pictures all around the box.

5. Have a number of people approximately ten years older than the children and thirty to fifty years older than the children to class as guests to be interviewed by the children who will use their note cards to guide their inquiry. Record some of the guests' answers on note cards and place them in the box with the pictures around it. (Students may conduct some interviews away from the school. They should take notes on the cards or record responses and then transfer ideas to the cards. Cards should then be placed in the box.)

6. Randomly select children to go to the box and pull out a card. Have students who didn't conduct the interview guess who the person is, what he or she likes to do (activities), and similarities and differences between this person's experiences and their own.

Evaluation: Keep an eye out for movies and television programs that focus on the lives of interesting people, older than the children in class, recom-

mend that children see these, and discuss them in class. Observe
student behavior, especially with regard to nonverbal communication with adults and peers.

Cultural Influences

Our discussion of the need for community leads us to a discussion of
cultural influences on people in communities. The concept "culture" has
been a key organizing term for teachers who have used the materials
developed in this book. The following lesson plan introduces this concept to students.

LESSON 44   WHAT IS A CULTURE?

Objectives: As a result of this lesson, students should be able to:

(1) define culture as a way of life whereby persons share many ideas as to
(a) the need for particular kinds of shelter, (b) preferences for acquiring,
preparing, and eating particular kinds of food, (c) preferences for particular kinds of clothing practices, and (d) preferences for particular
kinds of aesthetic, religious, and recreational practices; and

(2) discuss whether or not there really is such a thing as "a culture" and
give reasons for their position.

Methods and Materials:

1. Ask students to count off from one to six and instruct each group to
bring in a newspaper, magazine, or book picture that best answers the
following questions: (Each student can do this as a homework assign-
ment and then the group can select the picture it favors.)
   Group 1: What kind of shelter would you like to have?
   Group 2: What kind of food do you like best?
   Group 3: What clothes do you like best?
   Group 4: What kind of art, music, and writing do you prefer?
   Group 5: What religion do you like?
   Group 6: What kinds of recreation do you favor?

2. Have each group present its picture the following day and discuss why the group made this choice. (In some cases the group may wish to present more than one picture.)

3. Have the students consider the following generalization: "Although those of us in this class have some differences in what we like, there are also many similarities. In particular, there are some practices or kinds of behavior we would not consider to be acceptable."

   a. List the similarities on the board according to the items in the six questions and ask the students the name for the "way of life" this represents. Someone will probably say "culture."

4. Discuss whether or not there is such a thing as "a culture" if you feel the students are ready for this question. If some students are ready whereas others are not, have the students who are ready do a special assignment in answer to the question.

Evaluation: Observe student responses. Have a guest from another culture and see if students use their new knowledge in the discussion.

Comparing and contrasting are at the heart of elementary school learning. Similarities and differences within a culture were the main focus of the previous lesson plan. Similarities and differences between cultures are the subject of the following lesson plan:

LESSON 45   COMPARING CULTURES

Objectives: As a result of this lesson, students should be able to:

(1) identify some basic tasks common to all people;

(2) describe what is meant by the culture of a particular society; and

(3) compare and contrast briefly the culture of a particular society with their own.

Methods and Materials:

1. Choose three volunteers to go to the front of the room. Tell the three students that they are to pretend they are eating. Give one student chopsticks, the second silverware, and the third nothing. Instruct the student with the chopsticks to pretend he is eating rice and seaweed, the student with the silverware to pretend he is eating roast beef, and

the third student with no utensils to pretend he is eating whale blubber.

2. Ask the class a series of questions concerning what the three students are doing. Once they have identified the common task, eating, ask more specific questions as to what cultures or societies use such implements. Help the students, if necessary, in their inquiry. They should examine the generalization or hypothesis that although all students are performing the same task, the way in which this task is performed varies from culture to culture.

3. Choose three different students to role play. Instruct the three students that they are going to use different methods to seek food. Give one student a fishing net, the second a makeshift spear, and the third a shopping list.

4. Ask questions similar to the ones asked previously. Have the students consider the idea that although all people seek food, they fulfill this need in different ways from culture to culture.

5. Show the class a picture of an Eskimo family outside of their house and have the students compare their own housing conditions to those of the Eskimos. Have the students consider the generalization that all people have a basic need for shelter although they meet this need in different ways in different cultures.

6. Discuss what is meant by the term "culture."

Evaluation: Ask students to list other tasks common to all people and bring in for discussion any information they can gather about these tasks as a homework assignment.

The lesson plans on culture have been well received by both students and teachers. Students are especially interested in guessing what other students are doing in the front of the room. In this way, answers are not given away but rather they are discovered and articulated by the students themselves.

Language and communication patterns are interesting aspects of a culture, aspects that students can study. The general goal is to have students become aware of processes that they have simply taken for granted and not studied. We usually begin our lessons on communication with a learning experience that centers on nonverbal communication.

LESSON 46   VERBAL/NONVERBAL COMMUNICATION

Objectives: As a result of this lesson, students should be able to:

(1) identify and discuss the following generalizations: communication (expressing your thoughts and feelings so that others understand us and we in turn understand their expression of thoughts and feelings) depends on (a) the words we use, (b) body movement such as gestures and posture, (c) eye contact, and (d) attitudes of participants such as the desire to convey ideas and feelings; and

(2) explore the generalization that when people talk to each other they often change what they hear or leave out part of what they hear in communicating what they've experienced to others.

Methods and Materials:

1. Have students pair off and place their chairs back to back or sit on the floor back to back. Then say, "Sit straight, be very quiet, and don't turn your head. Think of the person behind you. Try to tell him something without talking." Then ask the question, "Did you understand what he was trying to tell you?" "Why?" (Students will probably say that they couldn't see or hear the person.)

2. Then say, "Now sit straight, don't turn your head, but try to talk to the person behind you." Add, "Did you understand what he was trying to tell you? Was it better than before?" "Why?" (Students will probably say that they had to shout and even then didn't communicate very well.)

3. Then say, "Now stand up, face each other, close your eyes, and talk to each other." In a few minutes add, "Did you understand what he or she tried to tell you? Was it still somewhat difficult?" "Why?" (Students will probably say they could not see the other person.)

4. Finally say, "Now open your eyes, stand up and talk to each other." Add, "How was this?" after a few minutes. Discuss the factors involved in good communication by listing students' responses on the board.

5. Have students form three equal lines. Tell them you are going to play the telephone game. Give the first person in line a message which he is expected to whisper to the next person in line and so on down the line. Ask the last person in line to say out loud what he or she heard. Do this with two or three messages and note changes in what is communicated. Ask students to discuss what happened to the first message.

(Students usually conclude that some people left out words and others changed words to give the message a different meaning.)

Evaluation: Note student responses. Ask students to watch a favorite television program, focus on one or two actors or actresses, and report to the class tomorrow on the topic "Why and how this person communicates well."

A teacher and her aide describe how the communication lesson was received in their classroom:

At the beginning we read the lesson plan and tried to think of how we might modify it. We considered several different ways to introduce the lesson and finally decided to begin with a movement activity. We asked the students to stand up and do the things we asked them to do: stretch real hard until it hurts your toes to stretch your arms so high; now wiggle like a tree does in the wind; and now jump as high as you can while staying in the same place on the floor. This eased the children into the communication activities. As the lesson began I could see that there was going to be some problem in hearing my directions if children didn't listen and so I introduced the rule that when my hand goes up all of us will close our mouths. This really helped the activity.

The interest level was high and the homework assignment really motivated them to try out their new learnings. We had a really interesting discussion of how television characters communicate and in the process I learned a lot about what programs and actresses and actors the students like to watch. Some of the parents mentioned the communication game at our P.T.A. meeting.

Children often find it difficult communicating with adults in a variety of settings: "He kept taking their money but he didn't even see me standing in line," one first grader said. "Sometimes I get the feeling that adults don't understand me," said a child who was yelled at by an adult in the neighborhood. The following lesson has been a useful springboard lesson to discuss communication problems between adults and children:

LESSON 47   COMMUNICATION PROBLEMS

Objectives: As a result of this lesson, students should be able to:

(1) define communication and what a communication problem means:

(2) give reasons for communication problems in the story and in their own lives; and

(3) suggest ways in which such problems can be solved.

Methods and Materials:

1. Read the following story to the children:

    Timmy is a five-year-old boy in a kindergarten class. He is very tall and people often think he is much older than five. At Christmas time he received some ice skates. He used them almost every day and soon became a good skater. At first Timmy's mother went with him to the outdoor ice rink, but lately he and his friends have gone there alone. One day Timmy's friends were busy after school and so Timmy went to the ice rink alone. When he got to the rink he found the shelter was closed and a sign was on the entrance to the rink. He didn't know what the sign said but he decided to put his skates on by the side of the rink. He skated for a while even though it wasn't much fun to skate alone.

    Suddenly he heard someone calling his name and he turned around to see the man who cares for the rink. Timmy waved and kept on skating doing all of the fancy tricks he had learned. Then he heard the man call again, "GET OFF THE ICE! CAN'T YOU READ THE SIGN?" Timmy knew the man wanted him to get off the ice and fast.

    He skated to the side of the rink and started to ask why he should get off the ice. The man didn't stop scolding long enough for Timmy to ask any questions. The man was angry and said, "A big boy like you should know how to read by now. Don't you understand?"

2. Ask the children in your class, "If you were in Timmy's place, how would you have felt?" Then ask, "If you were the man, how would you have felt?"

3. Ask the class if they know what the term *communication* means. Then ask if they know what the expression *communication problem* means. Ask for examples of communication problems they've experienced and ways they might have solved them.

Evaluation: Have each student come to class the following day with at least one communication problem and ways it can be solved. Observe student responses.

An early elementary school teacher used the lesson plan on communication problems and agreed to share her observations with us:

> I thought at first of the various kinds of communication children would be familiar with from their own experience: mail, the newspaper, television, radio, and telephone. I decided to use mail as a way to demonstrate communication that would involve each child. Since the lesson was about a boy named Timmy who couldn't read a sign, I put signs in a letter for each child—a picture of a stop sign, a no trespassing sign, a yield sign, and so on—so that each child would open his or her letter and have a special message. Then each child could read the letter and share its meaning with the class. For an introduction I decided to pretend to slip on the floor because I wasn't observant of a sign I borrowed from my custodian friend, Mr. Williams: CAUTION WET FLOOR. The introduction launched us into the lesson and the children loved opening their mail and reading their letters to the class.
>
> After the story the children related their ideas and feelings. They really felt sorry for Timmy and felt the man could have said what he had to say in a nicer way. At the same time they thought Timmy should not have gone skating alone.
>
> I decided during the lesson to ask students to notice signs on the way home and remember them for tomorrow. We had a good lesson the next day on signs they saw.

The teacher's experience with the communication problems lesson plan led her to construct a lesson plan on communicating without talking, based on an experience one of her children had.

LESSON 48   NONVERBAL COMMUNICATION

Objectives: As a result of this lesson, students should be able to:

(1) discuss the generalization that different forms of communication are appropriate for different times and different situations;

(2) define communication, verbal and nonverbal; and

(3) demonstrate that they can communicate nonverbally with others in the classroom and be aware of this process.

Methods and Materials:

1. Read the following story to the children:
   Carol is a five year old whose aunt and uncle are visiting. They will sleep in Carol's room so she must sleep in her baby sister's room. Before her mother puts Carol to bed, she says, "When you and anyone else go into the baby's room you must not make a sound or you will wake the baby."

2. Continue by saying, "Carol hears her father coming down the hall toward the baby's room in his heavy boots." How can Carol remind Daddy to be quiet? Remember she can't talk or she'll wake the baby.

3. The baby's room is cold. How can Carol tell her mother it is cold without talking?

4. Carol's mother brings a blanket and Carol feels warm now. How can she tell her mother without talking?

5. How can Carol's mother tell her she loves her without talking?

6. Point to a child in the classroom, gesture for the child to stand up, come to you, go back to his or her seat, and sit down. Discuss how all of this was done nonverbally.

Evaluation: Have children draw from a stack of cards on which are written directions for simple gestures. Let one child act out what is on the card and another guess what is being communicated. Examples are: I want to be your friend; I am mad at you; go away; come here; I am sleepy.

In discussing various kinds of communication, one student introduced the idea of citizens' band radios, a hobby he and his dad shared. The following lesson plan deals with this topic:

LESSON 49   COMMUNICATION NETWORKS

Objectives: As a result of this lesson, students should be able to:

(1) identify citizens' band radios as an example of an invention that helps people form informal communication networks;

(2) define *communication* and *networks;* and

(3) recognize that trade-offs within one's network help people get what they want at no financial cost.

Methods and Materials:

1. Inform students that you will play a voting game and if they answer the following questions with a "yes" they should raise their hands:
   a. How many of you have a CB radio in your home or car?
   b. How many of you have talked and listened to a CB radio?
   c. How many of you have heard people ask for help on the CB?
2. Have two students sit in the middle of a large circle of chairs and talk as if they were on CB radios during an "emergency" situation of their choice. Have other students take turns in doing this if you wish.
3. Ask students if CB radios are a formal or informal way of communicating. Help each other define formal and informal by listing examples under each category.
4. Ask students to name various reasons why people use CB radios. Discuss abuses as well as uses.
5. Introduce the concept *network* as an informal communication system whereby people exchange information and other resources (make trade-offs) at no financial cost.
   a. Ask students for more examples of network trade-offs, such as borrowing tools from neighbors, the sharing of child care, etc.

Evaluation: Observe student responses. Ask students to give examples of networks in other organizations including the school.

The previous lesson plan has stimulated a good deal of interest among students and teachers. In one classroom the students made CB posters designed to demonstrate how CBs can be useful in a variety of situations. Students have also compiled their own CB slang dictionaries in some classes. In the process they have talked about how language changes in a culture and how a new language is introduced. One class studied similarities and differences between truckers' use of CBs and the westward movement in the United States. In the process the role of the Federal Communications Commission was discussed. Interestingly enough, some students with a real understanding of CBs were not previously identified as good students. Their demonstrated knowledge of CBs was probably good for enhancing their self-concepts.

Understanding Organizational Influences

We are now in one of the most challenging areas of this book: How can we involve students in experiences that will lead them to new understandings about how organizations influence their lives? Students are so used to such influences that they take them for granted. In fact, they often act as if they aren't even conscious of how organizations influence them. Some students, particularly those rewarded by organizations such as the school, aren't about to question that which gives them special attention, for example in the form of grades and special privileges. Other students are so critical of organizations, although their criticism is often of a subtle nature, that they have dropped out in some way or another.

SUGGESTED ACTIVITIES

A good place to start in studying organizational influences is with a number of activities designed to find out what students presently know and feel and in the process launch them into new areas of inquiry. The following activities serve as examples:

1. Agree on a working definition of organization, such as a number of people who openly agree on certain goals and acceptable modes of behavior or ways of behaving.
2. The concepts developed earlier in this chapter are useful in raising questions about organizations: Do all organizations confine, sort, train, indoctrinate, and provide for personal means for self-development? Give examples to support your view on this matter.
3. Have students take a field trip to an organization very different from the school to study similarities and differences between this organization and the school.
4. Have the superintendent of schools come to your classroom and explain his perception of the school as an organization. Do likewise with a school board member and perhaps others interested in schools.
5. Have students interview people in various walks of life in order to get their perceptions of various organizations, such as the military, government, education, and voluntary organizations. Students should build an interview instrument ahead of time which should involve them in thought-provoking classes.
6. Study the classroom itself as an organization using concepts learned by the students.

The following lesson plan on "territoriality" can be useful in beginning your study of organizational influences:

LESSON 50   TERRITORIALITY

Objectives: As a result of this lesson, students should be able to:

(1) define *territoriality*;
(2) identify ways in which people and organizations "stake out their territories"; and
(3) identify ways in which they personally do this and react to others who do likewise.

Methods and Materials:

1. Have a table in the middle of a large circle with dinner place settings for four people with equal space for all. Ask four students to sit at the table.
2. Ask these students to leave the room for a minute after which you crowd three place settings into half of the table space while leaving the other half of the table for one person.
3. Ask the students to return to the room and sit in their chairs. Observe how the three students react to the crowded situation and discuss this with the class.
4. Introduce the concept "territoriality" as the psychological feeling that a particular space belongs to a person or group. Note that a person or group will try to defend this space from intruders.
5. Ask students for examples of how organizations "stake out their territory." Examples may include: security guards, alarm systems, fences, their own language systems (such as that used by a doctor or attorney).
6. Discuss how students feel about their "own" territory and the territory of organizations to which they belong. Have students explain ways in which their organizations "stake out their territory" and maintain their boundaries.
7. Ask, "How does our school do this?"

Evaluation: Read a case study of how an organization implements its territorial impulses. Compare and contrast human beings and other animals with regard to territorial matters.

The next lesson plan relates to organized hugeness in organizations. Specifically, the student is asked to personally relate his thoughts and feelings concerning large organizations.

LESSON 51   ATTITUDES TOWARD HUGE ORGANIZATIONS

Objectives: As a result of this lesson, students should be able to:

(1) define *huge organizations;*

(2) list the characteristics of large organizations, such as physical and psychological distance between members and the organization itself and its clients or constituents; and

(3) explore the generalization or hypothesis that "since large organizations make money off me in an impersonal way, I can 'bend the law' to make money off them."

Methods and Materials:

1. Read the following to the students:

   Mr. Jones accidentally ran into a small tree near his house and estimated the damage to be about $150. Since he had one-hundred-dollar-deductible insurance and would have to pay the first hundred dollars, he decided not to have the small dent in the front end of his car repaired.

   A month later Mr. Jones's car was hit by another car on his way to work. The trunk of his car was damaged quite a bit but the person at fault agreed to have his insurance company pay for repairs.

   While at the repair shop, Mr. Jones said to the manager, "While you're in the process of doing the rear of the car why don't you charge the insurance company to repair the dent in the front end of the car, but just write it down as a rear end repair."

2. If you were the manager of the repair shop, what would you say, knowing full well that your shop would make a greater profit by repairing the entire car and the insurance company wouldn't question the bill?

3. Does the size of the insurance company make any difference in your response? Does it make any difference if you know the owner of the insurance company or its representative?

4. Ask students for other examples of situations like the one in the case study.

5. Role play some of the situations in class and discuss what happened.

Evaluation: Observe student responses. Bring to class an article on a subject like the one in the lesson and ask for student responses.

Organizations often give the appearance of being objective, for their computer printouts and other electronic equipment look very official. It is important that students understand that very subjective decisions are made in spite of the appearance of objectivity. The following lesson plan on information summarizing makes this point:

LESSON 52   ASSESSING INFORMATION ABOUT ORGANIZATIONS

Objectives: As a result of this lesson, students should be able to:

(1) investigate the generalization that "many things done by organizations appear to be objective whereas in fact they are very subjective"; and
(2) become actively involved in exercising their views relating to organizations.

Methods and Materials:

1. Set the stage by informing the class that they will be executives for a large department store conglomerate that must make decisions regarding issuance of credit to customers. They will also have to make critical decisions with regard to the collection of monies from customers who haven't paid large bills.
2. Divide the class into groups with five persons per group. Give them the following assignment: It is your responsibility to identify five to ten items to be included on a credit form. The form will be an application for credit from your department store conglomerate.
3. Have each group present its items for class consideration. Debate controversial items.
4. Introduce the terms "objective" and "subjective" and develop a working definition in class. Then ask, "Do you believe that the decision to include particular items on a credit application form is objective or subjective? Explain."
5. Be sure to explain or explore the kinds of applicants who will be favored or disfavored by the items included. (For example, is it anybody's business whether or not your spouse works outside the home?)

6. Introduce the following critical incidents that each group will have to make decisions about in order to collect or not collect money from customers:

   a. A mother whose husband has left home and abandoned her five children is deeply in debt and she says she can't pay her three-hundred-dollar bill. What will you do?

   b. A young man of twenty-two has left the state and hasn't been heard from for four months. He owes the department store $900. What will you do?

   c. A sixty-year-old woman who owes $1,000 writes that she can't pay her bill due to the death of her husband who left her with nothing. She says that she simply isn't prepared to work herself because she has been out of the job market for so long and is in ill health with arthritis. What will you do?

   d. The minister of the church you attend owes the department store $600. He hasn't kept up his payments for three months and is about to move to another city. What will you do?

   e. I, the teacher of your class, owe $1,200 for a ride-on lawnmower I bought for my big lawn. I write you saying that the thing has never worked right and I refuse payment. What will you do?

Evaluation: Ask students to write an essay on objectivity and subjectivity in organizations. Have some read to the class.

Any person must learn to compromise or make tradeoffs in order to operate effectively in an organization. That is, a person who insists on having his or her own way all of the time will relate poorly to others in organizations, even if he or she owns the organization. The following lesson plan demonstrates the need for compromise in organizations.

LESSON 53   COMPROMISING WITHIN ORGANIZATIONS

Objectives: As a result of this lesson, students should be able to:

(1) discuss and take a position with regard to the generalization or hypothesis that "one must make some compromises in relating to others in organizations in order to be an effective decision-maker"; and

(2) examine and take a stand in relationship to "the myth of unlimited resources."

Methods and Materials:

1. Have the class form into four groups. Tell each group that it must choose a person to run for the office of Dispenser of Candy for the room. In five minutes another member of the group should be able to tell the whole class why its candidate should be elected Dispenser of Candy. After each group has presented its candidate to the class, a vote will be taken. Explain that if the class is able to elect a Dispenser of Candy by more than half the class voting for one candidate, the Dispenser of Candy will be allowed to dispense one piece of candy to each member of the class. The people who are members of the group whose candidate won the job will receive two pieces of candy. It will probably be necessary to take more than one vote and to allow some informal discussion time between the votes.

2. After the activity a discussion should be held centering around the idea that it was necessary to give up something, that is the two pieces of candy, in order to get any at all.

3. Write the word *myth* on the board and develop a working definition with the class. Then write the myth that "there are unlimited resources" on the board and discuss this myth in light of the learning activity just experienced. See if students conclude that the fact that there are limited resources means that each of us must compromise at times in order to be an effective decision-maker in an organization. If students don't bring this point of view into the discussion, introduce it yourself as a generalization or hypothesis to study.

Evaluation: Observe student responses during the activity. Ask students to bring to class newspaper articles that are relevant to their new learnings.

A second lesson on the need for compromise has been very successful when used by elementary school teachers.

LESSON 54   HOW DO YOU FEEL ABOUT COMPROMISES?

Objectives: As a result of this lesson, students should be able to:

(1) discuss and take a position with regard to the generalization or hypothesis that "one must make some compromises in relating to others in organizations in order to be an effective decision-maker"; and

(2) interview and analyze a recording of an interview with a public decision-maker on the topic "the need for compromise."

Methods and Materials:

1. Distribute to the class pieces of magazine pictures that have been cut in half and instruct them to have at least one completed picture in ten minutes, although not necessarily one of the pictures they were given.
2. Depending on the size of the group, it may be necessary to label the pictures as to who has the other half of the picture or letter the pictures so that the person holding the other half may be easily found.
3. The pictures should be distributed so that each student does not have a straight exchange with another student, but the pictures should be in units of three or four. Example—Student 1 has half of pictures A and C; Student 2 has half of B and D; Student 3 has half of A and B; and Student 4 has half of C and D.
4. The students should be allowed to form groups for five minutes or so to work out their exchanges and mount their pictures.
5. Then the class should discuss what they have done. Possible questions are:
   a. How was the problem of getting the other halves of the picture solved?
   b. What would have happened if others had not been willing to pool their pictures or at least been willing to give up one of their halves for a half that did not complete a picture?
   c. How do you feel about giving up something you have or want to someone else to achieve a desired goal?
6. Have students get into small groups after choosing a public figure they know for an interview on the topic "the need for compromise." Each small group will frame questions for the interview after which other groups will react to such questions.
7. Have each group conduct its interview and then analyze the recording from the cassette recorder. Their analysis and perhaps part of the tape should then be presented to the rest of the class for discussion.

Evaluation: Observe student responses, particularly as they build interview questions and analyze their tapes.

The compromise lessons have evoked lively responses from students. At the beginning of the lessons most students were very reluctant to compromise. After holding back for some time, they suddenly began trading in order to achieve their goals. Follow-up discussions of the lessons have frequently centered on what it means to be selfish or defend one's own interests. One student remarked, "If it helps me and others in the process it isn't selfish but it's simply good business." A classmate responded, "But if you always think of yourself first you may not help others at all." It is obvious from such discussions that students have received mixed signals from many sources, such as home, church, businesses, and school on the matter of interest in self and others. The compromise lessons can help the student sort through these mixed signals to arrive at his or her own conclusions.

The following lesson plan has been well received by students of all ages. In the process they have been introduced to the complexity of a growing organization.

LESSON 55   HENRY FORD BUILDS A CAR

Objectives: As a result of this lesson, students should be able to:

(1) sense the increased complexity that comes with an expanding or growing organization;
(2) define "division of labor";
(3) define "management" and "labor"; and
(4) suggest complexities of organizations within their own experience.

Methods and Materials:

1. Begin with the story of Henry Ford:
   Henry Ford didn't invent the automobile or car but he did mass produce it in factories in the United States. (Do any of you know what it means to mass produce something?) He began building his first car in a small garage in Detroit, Michigan. (How many of you are really interested in repairing cars and know something about car parts? Ask one student to join you in front of the room to demonstrate some of the decisions Henry Ford had to make.)
   Henry had car parts all over his garage. Some were on benches, some were on the floor, and some were hanging on the walls and from the ceiling. (Have the student volunteer name some car parts and scatter these parts around the room. Use books, objects, etc. to represent the parts.) Henry did so well with the first few cars that he decided he

needed a bigger place to build his cars and he wanted to have a more efficient place with many workers. (How should the workers be organized? For example, should a group of workers do one car and then move to another car to build it or should each worker have a specific job to do on an assembly line? Then ask, If you want an assembly line should you move or should the parts move to you? What level should the parts be at? Students will conclude that most parts should be at waist level so that you don't have to reach up or reach down all the time hurting your back.) Henry decided to interview many people for jobs. (Should he interview these people himself or have one of his men do it? What title should be given to this man?)

2. Introduce the concepts "management" and "labor" and have students dig up information on each for further discussion in class.
3. Also be sure that students understand the concept "division of labor."
4. Ask the student who is role playing Henry Ford if decisions are fewer or greater in number as his organization grows. Also ask him if he feels decisions are getting easier to make or harder to make. Introduce the term "complexity" and discuss organizational complexity. Ask students for examples they have from their own experience of organizational complexity. (For example, what are the differences between a neighborhood grocery store and a supermarket?)

Evaluation: Observe student responses. Bring a guest to class from a large organization and let students use their new knowledge in an interview situation.

The "Henry Ford Builds a Car" lesson plan has been especially successful with boys not identified traditionally as successful students. Many of these boys know a great deal about automobiles and they are interested in the lesson and love to tell others about their knowledge. It is quite a learning experience for the teacher too for he or she finds out how much students know about cars.

Conclusion

The title of this part, "And You Make Two . . . and More . . . ," indicates the importance of others in our lives. In the first section of this part a number of self-inventories aided us in relating to three themes: (1) the need for community, (2) cultural influences on our relationships with others, and (3) organizational influences on our relationships with others. In the second section of this part the reader was exposed to various learning experiences designed to implement the ideas from the first part.

It should be clear at this point that when teachers experience success in classrooms they feel good about relating to themselves and others, which is another way of saying that each person nurtures the "wonderful me" within him or her. In the next part we will turn to relationships among ourselves, others, and the environment in which we live, an environment whose fragility has recently come into our consciousness. This part is titled "... on Planet Earth."

NOTES

1. Seymour Sarason, *The Psychological Sense of Community* (San Francisco: Jossey-Bass, 1974), p. 1.

2. *Ibid.*, pp. 1—2.

3. *Ibid.*, p. 143.

4. Dorothy Lee, *Freedom and Culture* (Englewood Cliffs, N.J.: Prentice-Hall, 1959), p. 76.

5. Seymour Sarason, *Work, Aging, and Social Change* (New York: The Free Press, 1977).

6. Dale L. Brubaker, *Creative Leadership in Elementary Schools* (Dubuque, Iowa: Kendall/ Hunt, 1976). The thesis of the book is that teachers should assume professional responsibility for decisions in the areas of curriculum and instruction. The last two chapters describe two schools where teachers met this challenge.

7. Dale L. Brubaker and Roland H. Nelson, Jr., *Introduction to Educational Decision-Making* (Dubuque, Iowa: Kendall/Hunt, 1972), pp. 47—71.

8. For a discussion of adult involvement in schools see Chapter 8, "The Parent and the Adult Community Participant," in Brubaker, *Creative Leadership in Elementary Schools*, pp. 127—36.

PART THREE

...on Planet Earth

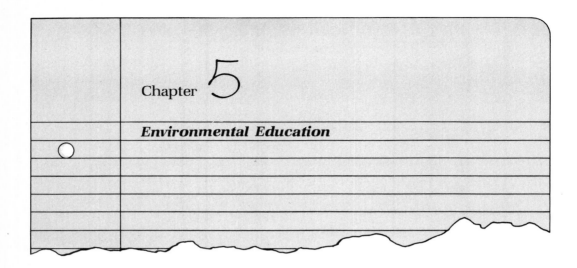

Chapter 5

Environmental Education

A kind of revolution has taken place in the last decade: we are conscious of the fact that our physical environment deeply influences people, communities, organizations, and cultures. Before this awareness occurred, the majority of people in technologically advanced cultures considered all technetronic discoveries a boon to the quality of life each of us would experience: bigger and more elaborate cars, airplanes, and houses, for example, were necessarily considered better. The myth of unlimited progress was complemented by the myth of unlimited resources. These myths were shared by most people in advanced technological areas of the world for their domains had more natural resources than the less advanced areas. Within the advanced technological areas of the world, those people with the greatest resources had the most political potency. The disenfranchised in our urban slums and rural pockets of poverty were simply ignored.

It was natural that our institutions, organizations, and communities reflected attitudes discussed in the previous paragraph. The attitude that provided the cement that held all other attitudes together was that man could conquer the environment through his own efforts, which is to say in effect that people and the environment are separate or discrete entities often in conflict. Listen to the following view of today's environmentalist, a marked contrast to the social Darwinist position previously discussed: *we hope to teach children and others that all living things are interdependent and connected with each other and the environment.* We grow emotionally in sharing with each other and the environment. We grow in harmony with each other and the environment by recognizing relatedness. This reminds us of our previous discussions of what it means to be centered.

Now that we recognize the difficulties created by our traditional attitude toward the environment, we have responded in a variety of ways. A few people would have us just leave everything alone in the hope that over a period of time nature will take its own course. Most people, however, emphasize the mixed results of technological changes: they want to keep the basic advance, such as the automobile, but they want to eliminate some things, such as automobile "fins" and other similar frills, and correct others. How do they intend to make such corrections? Largely through technology as reflected in terms such as "environmental management." In the process of involving ourselves in environmental management, we have explored and begun to understand our relationship with the environment. In particular, we realize that certain conflicts are inevitable: those who "own" the land, for example, express desires that sometimes conflict with desires of public environmental managers; economic efficiency and conservation of a natural resource are often at odds; people's wants and needs aren't always synonymous for they sometimes need what they don't want and at other times want what they don't need; and people's interpretations of moral responsibility with respect to the environment differ. The process of conflict resolution or reconciliation is often cloaked in the language of rights and responsibilities. At times such rhetoric finds its way into the courts for legal settlement. For example, in what space or spaces do people have the right to smoke and what responsibilities do they have in order to respect the rights of those whose space is violated by polluted air? Or, what rights and responsibilities are involved when a beer company wants to produce pop-top cans, a process which would produce jobs for many in a poor rural setting? These are the issues that provide the grist for the mill of active learning in elementary schools.

Now that the complexity and challenge of environmental education have been introduced, let us turn to a self-inventory that will lead us into the area of instruction for children in elementary schools.[1]

SELF-INVENTORY 10

1. Do you believe the natural environment can be replaced?
   _____ _____ Please explain your answer.
       Yes   No

   _____

   _____

   _____

2. Do you believe that *all* living things evolve and change?
   _____ _____ Please explain by giving examples.
       Yes   No

   _____

   _____

   _____

3. Do you believe that it is accurate to say that altering the natural
   environment involves risk taking and that those who do it should be
   aware of this? _____ _____ Given your position on this issue, fur-
                      Yes   No
   nish examples from your neighborhood to illustrate your point of
   view.

   _____

   _____

   _____

4. In what ways, if any, must those involved in environmental management relate to the issue of increased population?

   _____

   _____

   _____

5. Please give examples of the relationship between technological changes and social changes. Where possible, explain how you were personally influenced by such changes.

_____

_____

_____

6. Do you believe that environmental management sometimes involves just leaving things alone? _____ _____ Please give examples to
   Yes   No
   support your views.

_____

_____

_____

7. We have been taught that there are many causes for any event (multiple causation). Do you believe that sometimes we don't know any causes for an event (no known causation)? _____ _____ Explain by
giving examples to support your position.   Yes   No

_____

_____

_____

What are the implications of your position on this matter for environmental education?

_____

_____

_____

8. What are the implications of increased leisure time for involving yourself in environmental education?

_____

_____

_____

9. In what ways, if any, should those involved in environmental management consider architecture in their plans?

_____

_____

_____

What are the implications of your answer for you, a teacher, in relating
to school architecture, including landscape architecture?

_____

_____

_____

10. What role does public opinion play in environmental education?

_____

What are some of the ways you and your students can influence
public opinion concerning your views on environmental education?

_____

_____

_____

11. What evidence do you see that still supports the myth that all technetronic discoveries lead to "progress"?

_____

_____

_____

Give examples of inventions and new products that you would like to see banned.

_____

_____

_____

12. What evidence do you see that still supports the myth that there are unlimited resources?

_____

_____

_____

13. In what ways, if any, has the community in which you live successfully managed the environment rather than exploited it?

_____

_____

_____

In what ways has the community exploited the environment?

_____

_____

_____

14. What progress has your *class* made in the area of environmental education and what still might be done?

_____

_____

_____

15. What progress has your *school* made in the area of environmental education and what still might be done?

_____

_____

_____

Chapter 6

We're All In It Together

Two major goals governed the selection of materials for this chapter: the materials should integrate ideas from the first two parts, and the materials should demonstrate the theme that people are related or connected to their environment when their emotions are centered. The first and second goals depend on each other, as evidenced in the part titles of this book, WONDERFUL ME . . . AND YOU MAKE TWO . . . AND MORE . . . ON PLANET EARTH. No part of this title can really stand alone, given the basic assumptions that guided the writing of this book.

The goals for this chapter were also helpful in serving as a filter for the selection of materials, given a major dilemma regarding the decision as to what to include and exclude. The dilemma is a fortunate one for it is simply that there is a tremendous reservoir of materials from which one can choose. The reader can find plenty of previously published material on the market. Materials in this section have not been published before, but were constructed to fit into the organization of this book and serve as springboards for teachers to use in settings of their choice.

Energy Conservation

Our awareness of limited natural resources has greatly increased in the last few years with government and business leaders sometimes working together in ways that would have been inconceivable two or three decades ago. The following lesson plan was written in order to bring students' attention to energy or power.

LESSON 56   LEARNING ABOUT ENERGY

Objectives: As a result of this lesson, students should be able to:

(1) explain that all plants and animals need energy to live and grow;
(2) identify the source of energy for plants, animals, cars, and appliances; and
(3) explain why the sun is so important to plants and animals.

Methods and Materials:

1. Begin by asking the students what a hamburger, gasoline, a milkshake, and electricity have in common. (Someone will probably say that all provide energy in some way to the things that use or consume them.)
2. Draw a picture of the sun on the blackboard. Explain that the sun provides much of the energy that people, animals, and plants need to live and grow. This is because the light (energy) from the sun gives the leaves the energy to make their own food. Since people and animals can't make their own food, they eat plants or the meat from other animals to get their energy.
3. Ask the students if cars get their energy from plants. If students say no because cars get their energy from gasoline, explain that gasoline comes from really very, very old plants that got their energy from the sun. Explain that millions of years ago plants died and then their leaves were buried under the ground. After millions of years the dead leaves changed into oil which contains the gasoline that provides energy to run our cars.
4. Ask the students if all energy comes from the sun. Keep in mind that water is a source of energy that doesn't come from the sun. An example

is water rushing over a dam turning large turbines that generate electricity that gives us energy for lights at home, power for appliances, etc.

5. Find pictures from a magazine of a cow, a person, a gas-powered lawnmower, a push lawnmower, and a goat. Hold up each picture, one at a time, and ask the students how each gets energy to do its work. For example, a cow gets its energy from grass, grain, and other feed; a person gets energy from food (milk, meat, bread, etc.); a gas-powered lawnmower gets its energy from gas; a push lawnmower gets its energy from the person pushing it; and a goat from just about anything for it eats a variety of things. Ask the students if they ever thought of themselves as a source of energy.

Evaluation: Observe how the students identify sources of energy for plants, animals, and fuel powered machines. Have the students suggest other kinds of energy, such as steam, coal, nuclear, wind, etc.

Young children usually take pride in conserving energy at school and at home. Once they get in the habit of conserving energy, they find new ways to help their parents, teachers, and others do likewise. The following lesson plan focuses on saving energy at home.

LESSON 57   CONSERVING ENERGY IN THE HOME

Objectives: As a result of this lesson, each student should be able to:

(1) discuss ways to conserve electricity in the home;
(2) suggest ways to conserve natural gas in the home;
(3) tell why these methods of conservation are effective; and
(4) help save money on utility bills by applying these methods of conservation in the home.

Methods and Materials:

1. Give the following assignment one week in advance of the lesson. Assignment: Ask your parents how much the electricity and/or gas bill was for the previous month. Explain that the class is studying ways to conserve energy. Ask if your parents feel conserving energy could help cut the price of your utility bills. Observe ways in which energy is wasted in your home for a week, record such information, and bring it to class in a week.

2. After a week's observation at home, ask the students to raise their hands if they think they could cut their utility bills through energy conservation.
3. List on the board ways in which energy is wasted in homes.
4. Have each child tear a piece of paper in half and write "electricity" at the top of one sheet and "gas" at the top of the other sheet. Have each child list five ways his family could save electricity on one sheet and five ways his family could save gas on the other.
5. Have children share their lists with others in the class if they wish. List on the board ways to save electricity and gas and discuss ideas using some of the following questions:
   a. Can we avoid using lights during daylight hours?
   b. Name different appliances available for purchase today. How necessary are these appliances?
   c. How can storm windows and doors aid in conserving heat in the winter and cool air in the summer?
   d. Why should the thermostat remain at one temperature?
   e. How can insulation help conserve heat?
   f. What is a pilot light? How can this help conserve energy?

Evaluation: Ask the children to write an essay in which they discuss what happened when they tried to conserve energy at home. Have them draw a picture of the inside of their homes to indicate places where they conserved energy. Ask if they saved any money after a month or more of conserving energy.

A critical incident in the lives of the children can often act as a springboard for a lesson on energy conservation, as the following lesson plan demonstrates.

LESSON 58   PREPARING FOR LOSS OF ELECTRICITY

Objectives: As a result of this lesson, students should be able to:

(1) discuss changes in one's lifestyle as a result of electrical power loss (outage);
(2) identify those items that all persons should have in the event of an outage;

(3) list ways in which persons can cooperate in the event of such an outage; and

(4) set priorities for restoring power.

Methods and Materials:

1. Inform the students that you will list on the board some of the things
that would happen to each member of the class if an ice storm caused
the loss of electricity for several days.

2. Place a large trunk or box in the front of the room with its contents not
visible to students. The trunk or box should contain items needed for a
power outage. Ask students to guess what you've placed in the trunk or
box and list these things on the board.

3. Have one student open the trunk or box and place items guessed cor-
rectly on a desk. (Items might include matches, candles, a flashlight, a
battery-powered radio, a first-aid kit, a fire extinguisher, warm blankets
or sleeping bags, warm clothes, and food that requires no cooking or
refrigeration.) Discuss the possible uses of each item.

4. Discuss ways in which people can cooperate in the event of a power
outage.

5. Have students prepare a newsletter for parents containing a list of essential items in the event of an outage. Have each student take the
newsletter home and also hand out the newsletter at the P.T.A. monthly
meeting.

6. Ask the students to set priorities for work crews who will restore power.
Students may include hospitals, rest homes, power companies, telephone companies, churches, schools, restaurants, and supermarkets. If
they don't include one or more of these places, introduce them yourself.

7. Ask students what they would do if they saw a broken electrical wire
near their home.

Evaluation: Observation of student responses. Listen to adult responses to the
student project. Have students discuss what the school should do
in the event of an outage.

The next lesson on saving trees touches students' emotions and
involves them in practical ways to conserve our forests.

LESSON 59   SAVE THAT TREE!

Objectives: As a result of this lesson, students should be able to:

(1) give reasons for the importance of recycling paper, especially news-papers; and

(2) suggest practical ways in which they can help in this enterprise.

Methods and Materials:

1. Bring to class a variety of products made from trees focusing largely on paper products ranging from heavy cardboard to Kleenex tissues. Give a simplified explanation of how paper is made from trees if a student can't do so.

2. Ask what would happen in the following hypothetical situation. People use so many paper products and wood that forests were cut down without those who used the products knowing it. The following questions might guide the discussion that follows:

    a. What do you think might happen as a result of this matter?
    b. What would happen if we ran out of trees?
    c. How would it affect us if we didn't have any paper?
    d. What kinds of paper products can be recycled?
    e. How can your family save paper for recycling?
    f. How else can we save trees?

Evaluation: Listen to responses of the children and then have them make an ecology poster stressing reasons for recycling or showing ways they can participate. Take children to a recycling plant if one is nearby. Have children suggest ways they can provide leadership for saving trees.

SUGGESTED ACTIVITIES

1. Get information on the recycling of aluminum cans, have students collect cans, and have a field trip to weigh cans at the nearby collection station.

2. Build newspaper collection boxes for each child's home, collect papers, and involve fathers and mothers in taking children and papers to a collection station where papers will be weighed.

3. Have students make posters urging people not to use paper bags in purchasing most items from stores.

4. Meet on a Saturday at the school with the children and parents and plant trees and shrubbery.

5. Make posters that suggest ways to conserve water at home. Include items such as repairing dripping faucets, taking short showers rather than long showers, shallow rather than deep baths, and the like.

6. Construct posters that demonstrate the proper use of fireplaces.

7. Distribute bricks for people to place in water reservoirs of toilets or recommend changing the reservoir float height to save water. Toilets use approximately five gallons of water every time they are flushed.

8. Construct posters that urge people to buy soft drinks, beer, and milk in returnable bottles. They are often cheaper this way, too.

9. *Distribute all posters in strategic areas of the community.*

Fighting Pollution

Those who pollute threaten our environment and in the process waste energy. Antipollution campaigns have taken many forms in many parts of the nation. In this section we will include lessons and learning experiences designed to help children and the teacher become more aware of what happens when we pollute the air, the water, and the land. Such awareness should be followed by a commitment to activities that will help fight pollution. The first lesson plan, "L.J. Builds a Treehouse," integrates many learnings from previous parts of this book.

LESSON 60   L.J. BUILDS A TREEHOUSE[2]

Objectives: As a result of this lesson, students should be able to:

(1) discuss ecological considerations, such as whether or not to drive nails into a tree, the location of a tree house, and the appearance of the treehouse when completed;

(2) make decisions with respect to cooperation and competition with peers and adults, including parents; and

(3) make decisions with respect to "in groups" and "out groups."

Methods and Materials:

1. Read the following story to the children or have one (or more) of the children read it, stopping where appropriate for questions and discussion.

L.J. is seven and will be in third grade next fall. Everyone calls him L.J. for Little John. This is so people don't mix him up with Big John, his father.

L.J. has a four-year-old brother and a sister who is starting to walk. She gets into everything.

L.J. has a huge backyard with tall, tall trees. He wants to build a treehouse more than anything else. (Should he talk to his father and mother before he builds a treehouse?)

L.J. talks to his parents about the treehouse. (Which of these might Little John be told: A. You can't do it! B. You may do it in the big tree way back in the corner of the yard! C. You may build it anywhere in the backyard! D. You may build it if Mike, your brother, can help!)

Big John tells L.J., "You may use the old lumber in the backyard." Four-year-old Mike follows L.J. into the backyard. He wants to help. (Is there anything Mike could do?)

L.J.'s first job is to pick a tree. Does he want a tall tree, a fat tree, or just a medium tree? Will the tall tree hold the big treehouse? L.J. says "No! Ah ha! The medium tree is tall enough and strong enough and easy to climb. That's where we'll build the treehouse!"

L.J. asks Mike to help him carry some of the long boards. It will be a big job to get all the lumber into the right place. Some of the lumber is too heavy for even L.J. and Mike. Big John won't be home for hours but mother just came home. L.J. and Mike see Barbara. She is one of the biggest girls in fifth grade. (Should L.J. and Mike ask Barbara to help?) Barbara walks slowly into the yard. She asks L.J. if she can get a hammer and help build the treehouse. (What should L.J. say?)

It is now time to begin building the treehouse and L.J. asks himself a question, "What will happen to the tree if I pound nails into it? Will it hurt the tree?" (What do you think about this? Is there some other way L.J. can build the treehouse without using nails that go into the tree?)

Big John comes home and suggests that L.J. and Mike place the boards in places in the tree where nails won't have to be pounded into the tree. Big John also uses big ropes to hold the main boards in place. The problem now is that Big John is so involved in the treehouse that L.J. has nothing to do. (What should L.J. say?)

After dinner, L.J. and Mike start working again on the treehouse. Soon they run out of lumber. L.J. thinks he should use his own money to buy new lumber. Mike thinks they should take the lumber from a new house next door. Big John thinks they should ask the man next door if he has any extra lumber that he doesn't want to use because it isn't perfect. (What would you do?)

L.J. and Mike finish the treehouse and discuss how it looks. L.J. says, "I wonder if we should paint it green so it looks like the trees and can't be seen as well." Mike adds, "It shouldn't stick out like a sore thumb." (What do you think about this? What would you do?)

L.J. and Mike are really proud of their treehouse. L.J. and Mike decide they want a club. They make a sign that says GIRLS KEEP OUT! (What do you think of this?)

Carol and Barbara want to join the club. Carol is their little sister. Barbara helped with the work. (Should the girls be allowed to join?)

The boys still won't let any girls in the club. Barbara says the treehouse is half hers. She helped build it. (What would you say to Barbara?)

Dean is a friend of Mike and Barbara. He wants to play in the treehouse. L.J. does not like Dean. Dean and L.J. often fight. Mike will never play in the treehouse unless Dean can play there too. (What should L.J. do?)

An early elementary school teacher found "L.J. Builds a Treehouse" a stimulating lesson for herself and the children in her classroom. She describes her experience with the lesson as follows:

Before I began reading the story I asked the children some questions about their experiences with treehouses: "Has anyone ever built one?" If you did, what kind of tree did you use?" "Did you get any help from your friends in building the treehouse?" These questions gave the children a chance to tell me about their own neighborhoods which I knew little about before this. The questions also motivated them to be interested in the story I was about to tell.

One of the things that really got the story off on the right foot was to bring in a picture of a treehouse children in our neighborhood had built. I took the picture and had it enlarged. After showing it to the children I put it on our bulletin board.

One thing I should have expected but didn't was the amount of attention the children would give to safety as a factor in building a treehouse. One child said, "My parents wouldn't let me build a treehouse unless I built it on the ground." I said to myself, "What kind of a *tree*house would that be?" Children were also concerned about safety in using a hammer and they were worried about getting splinters from the boards.

The children really got involved in the story and had lots of questions of their own.

Evaluation: Observe student responses. Have students draw pictures of similar experiences and explain their pictures to other students in the class.

"Looking for Bottles" is another lesson plan that integrates the many themes we've developed in this book, including pollution and its influence on our lives.

LESSON 61 LOOKING FOR BOTTLES

Objectives: As a result of this lesson, students should be able to:

(1) discuss the results of pollution, particularly land pollution, and how recycling of glass can conserve energy and stop this particular kind of pollution;

(2) be conscious of commitments they make with regard to facing this issue in their lives;

(3) decide the extent to which they wish to share and cooperate in fighting pollution and also share in the profits for returning "returnable bottles"; and

(4) decide how they would relate to adults if faced with decisions like those in the story.

Methods and Materials:

1. Read or have one or more of the students read the following story, pausing where appropriate for questions and discussion.

   Jim is a second grader and has a sister in the first grade. Jim got a new bike a year ago. It is yellow with a big wire basket on the front handlebars for carrying things.

   One day Jim got an idea: "Why not pick up returnable bottles in the neighborhood and make some money! It would also help fight pollution by getting rid of litter and kids won't cut themselves on the glass." (Should Jim ask his parents before he starts picking up bottles?)

   Jim takes his bike and starts collecting bottles. (If workmen are near the new houses where bottles are littered, should Jim ask them if he can take the bottles? Should Jim collect beer bottles as well as pop bottles? As some bottles are marked *Not Returnable*, which means you don't get money for returning them, should Jim also pick up these bottles? Discuss pollution and recycling of glass and other products as a means for fighting pollution.)

   Jim's sister wants to bring her wagon along and help Jim collect bottles. (What should Jim say?)

   Jim's friend Billy wants to bring his bike along and help collect bottles.

(What should Jim say?)

Jim's friend would get half the money and Billy likes the idea a lot. Jim agrees. (What do you think is fair?)

Jim and Billy find out at the store that they get one cent less for dirty bottles. (Should they clean the bottles? If so, how?)

Jim gets his dad to take a walk and see where he (Jim) gets his bottles. His dad helps Jim get a lot of bottles from the houses where workmen have been working. (Should Jim offer to pay his dad some of the money he makes when he returns the bottles?) Jim collects a lot of bottles. (About how many should Jim collect each time before taking them to the store? How should Jim store the bottles? Remember that glass breaks easily. How should Jim keep a record of the number of bottles he collects each time? In his head (memory)? On paper?)

Jim and his father drive to the store with the bottles. (Who should talk to the clerk at the cash register? Jim? His father? Both of them?)

Evaluation: Observe student responses. Have students draw a picture to show what they learned. The picture, it should be explained, is a symbol of what they learned. Have each student explain his symbolic picture.

A fourth grade teacher used "Looking for Bottles" with her children and describes in the following paragraphs the results of her experience.

At the time we were dealing with this lesson, there was a controversy in a nearby town about a new bottling plant and so I summarized the controversy and asked the students to react to it:

A brewing company wants to buy 60 acres of land in the outskirts of the nearby community. The company would use the land to construct a can factory for its beer. Production would be 500 million 12-ounce cans and 250 million 16-ounce cans each year. All cans would be made of aluminum. The company would hire approximately 350 people.

A number of citizens in the state have drafted a law that would prohibit sale of disposable cans and bottles containing beer and soft drinks. They argue that disposable bottles pollute land and streams and lakes in the region and furthermore are a safety hazard, for many people are cut by these containers each year.

I asked the students: "What is your position with regard to (1) the location of the brewing company's new plant in the community, and (2) the proposed law banning the sale of disposable beer and soft drink cans and bottles?"

The case study and questions involved the students in heated debates with the main issue being the creation of jobs and at the same time increased pollution. I wondered how much the students reflected their parents' views in our discussions.

After reading the lesson, I decided that I wanted to build some of my own ideas into it. I therefore put on an old shirt with "litterbug" written on it and came into the classroom throwing paper on the floor, leaving my bottles on the floor, and talking all the time about how it's OK to litter. This caught the students' attention and they couldn't understand what this was all about.

Most of the children were aware of the consequences of pollution and the need for safe and effective means of collecting bottles. They were very familiar with terms such as recycling, returnable, nonreturnable, no deposit-no return, no-refill, money-back bottle, and pollution. I believe the fact that they knew what these terms meant gave them confidence in dealing with the lesson. They expressed their thoughts readily. The students were interested in different ways to wash bottles so that they would get more money. They were also very much aware of the importance of safety precautions with bottles. One boy said that he would collect the bottles, wash them, and return them himself to get *all* the money. I asked him, "Wouldn't you be lonely not having someone to talk to?" He responded, "I'd talk to the lady at the grocery store!" I thought that was a good response and I realized that I had tried to impose my values on him, but he felt free to disagree.

In spite of extensive campaigns to prevent littering, one still finds litter along beautiful winding roads and trails as well as along more widely used thoroughfares. The following lesson plan reminds children of the littering problem.

LESSON 62   DOWN WITH THE LITTERBUG!

Objectives: As a result of this lesson, students should be able to:

(1) define littering;
(2) decide if littering is right or wrong and support their conclusion;
(3) list problems caused by littering; and
(4) suggest and involve themselves in activities that will prevent littering.

Methods and Materials:

1. Gather together poster paper, magic markers, paint, and empty barrels or boxes.
2. Read the following story to the class or have one or more of the students read the story:

   It was a beautiful summer day. Jeff and Steve decided to go for a ride on their bikes. They rode out into the country, by the green field and pastures. They decided to stop by a quiet pond and eat their sandwiches. After they ate, Jeff walked up to the pond, crumpled up his paper bag, and tossed it into the pond because there wasn't a trash can nearby. Steve said, "Jeff, you shouldn't throw paper into the pond 'cause it makes it look ugly." Jeff responded, "Aw, Steve, it's all right 'cause everybody does it." He added, "Look at all the trash floating around and lying on the banks." For the first time, Steve looked around him and noticed all the trash lying around.
3. Begin the discussion by asking the following questions:
   a. What is the word for what Jeff did?
   b. How does Jeff feel about littering? How does Steve feel about it? How do you feel about it and why?
   c. Is it all right to litter since everybody else does it? Is it all right to litter if there isn't a trash can nearby? What else could you do with the paper?
   d. What are some of the problems littering can cause?
   e. Can you think of a place nearby where there is a lot of litter?
   f. What can we do to remind people not to litter?
   g. What can we do about litter that is already here?
4. Have the children get actively involved in the campaign against litter by:
   a. Getting some empty barrels and boxes, painting and decorating them, and then placing them around the schoolyard as trash cans.
   b. Getting some poster paper and magic markers and letting the children make "don't litter" posters and place them around the school and in stores in the community.
   c. Have children go outside and pick up trash on the playground and put it in bags.

Evaluation: Observe student responses with particular attention to whether or not they litter themselves and tell others not to litter.

Unique features of the area in the region near the school can be the subject for ecology lessons that teach children not to pollute. A swamp near the school is the subject of the next lesson.

LESSON 63   THE SWAMP

Objectives: As a result of this lesson, students should be able to:

(1) gain confidence that comes with participation in community decision making;
(2) express a personal opinion backed by reasons for the opinion;
(3) organize these reasons into an argument for presentation to others; and
(4) make a decision regarding issues discussed after hearing a variety of views on the subject.

Methods and Materials:

1. Read the following to the students or have one or more of them read it: You are a resident of Swamptown. Just outside the boundaries of the town is a large swamp. This swamp provides many homes for birds and other animals. However, some people have recently been dumping old furniture and other similar objects and garbage into the swamp. The acres of land beneath the swamp could also be used for a new industry that would employ approximately 450 people.

   As a resident you have to decide how to deal with people who are dumping their trash in the swamp and you must also decide what to do about the new industry proposed for the swamp site.

   Please divide into groups of five and recommend ways to (1) identify and (2) deal with people who are dumping trash in the swamp. Next, discuss your options on the ballot regarding the proposed new industry: (1) drain the swamp and let the industry buy the land for its buildings; or (2) leave the swamp as it is, thus preserving the homes of the birds and animals. Divide the class according to whether they prefer option (1) or (2). Then have each side enter into a debate after organizing their reasons into a clear case for their position.

   After the debate is over, have the students meet as a large group and vote again by secret ballot.

2. Discuss what happened with the students. Especially discuss the role of some students in persuading others.

Evaluation: Observe students as they participate in this lesson. Give particular attention to students' ability to organize arguments and then present them.

Water pollution is the result of our careless relationship with the environment. The following lesson plan makes clear the values that are in conflict when we pollute our waterways.

LESSON 64   WATER POLLUTION

Objectives: As a result of this lesson, students should be able to:

(1) identify some causes of water pollution;
(2) weigh courses of action to be taken when one observes water being polluted; and
(3) identify values in conflict when water is being polluted.

Methods and Materials:

1. Read the following story and pause when appropriate for questions and discussion:

   Randy, a ten year old, lives about five miles out of town. There is a river that runs through his father's farm. In past years there was a special "swimming hole" where he and some of his friends swam during the summer.

   Last summer when they went swimming, they began to notice debris occasionally floating near the edge of the water. The water had a bad odor at times and occasionally Randy saw a dead fish going downstream. The boys really liked swimming there. Randy knew that if they told his father he would make them stop swimming in the river.

   a. Should Randy tell his father anyway even though he probably will not be allowed to swim in the river? Or, should Randy keep on swimming there and not tell his father?

   b. What if one of Randy's friends gets sick, with the polluted water as a possible cause? What should Randy do?

   c. What should Randy do about the fish that are dying?

   Dave, Randy's twelve-year-old cousin, visited on the farm this last summer. When Randy and Dave went to the swimming hole, a lot of litter could be seen in the water and many more dead fish were floating on top. Dave told Randy about the factories in town which dump sewage and chemicals in the river. Randy hadn't heard about this before. His dad works in one of the factories which Dave says dump these chemicals in the river.

    a. Should Randy ask his dad to stop working in the factory? Should Randy even discuss this matter of factories polluting the river and pond with his father?

    b. If Randy's father quit his job, how would his family live?

2. Continue the discussion with the students to see ways in which they can fight water pollution in their communities.

Evaluation: Observe student responses. Ask each student to write an essay on "Water Pollution and What I Will Do About It." Have students write letters to government officials who make decisions concerning clean water.

Air pollution is the subject of the next lesson. Children who live in areas with serious air pollution problems will need no introduction to the subject, but students who live in areas with clean air may not yet be acquainted with the topic "air pollution."

LESSON 65   AIR POLLUTION

Objectives: As a result of this lesson, students should be able to:

    (1) define pollution in general and air pollution in particular;

    (2) identify the major causes of air pollution;

    (3) identify ways the person can help prevent air pollution; and

    (4) list the effects of air pollution on our world and on each of us.

Methods and Materials:

1. In order to get students' attention and motivate them, show pictures of factories spewing waste into the air and of cars polluting the air.

2. Read the following story to the class:

Not so very long ago, there were no cars or factories. People rode horses and horse-pulled carriages and they made the things for themselves that factories now make for us. Then, people started making easier ways to get these things done. They invented cars and factories. There were problems though because cars burn gasoline which produces carbon monoxide. This is harmful to humans who breathe it. With so many cars around, more and more carbon monoxide is let into the air. Factories burn fuels too and the smoke from them entered the air. In the big cities people started noticing the air was filled with smoke and fog, called smog. The smog didn't blow away and made it hard to breathe. Factory owners and car makers finally realized that they were going to have to take responsibility for trying to clean the air.

3. Ask some of the following questions:
   a. What causes air pollution?
   b. Are there other causes than those in the story?
   c. Has there always been dirty air?
   d. Do some places have dirtier air than others? Why?
   e. What can we as individuals do to help fight air pollution?
   f. What are government leaders, factory owners, and car makers doing to help solve the problem? What else should they do?
   g. What would happen if nothing were done?
4. Continue the discussion with the students noting their preconceptions, biases, and attitudes toward pollution in general and air pollution in particular.
5. Invite government officials responsible for clean air leadership into your classroom and have students interview them after organizing questions beforehand.
6. Have the class work together in order to write letters to government leaders on the subject of fighting air pollution.

Evaluation: Have students draw "before pollution" and "after pollution" pictures. Have them identify sources of air pollution in their own community and make commitments to remedy the problem.

Technetronic advances, such as those in the aviation industry, have called our attention to noise pollution. Factory workers are often subject to noises that can cause hearing problems. The following lesson plan introduces children to the subject of noise pollution.

LESSON 66   NOISE POLLUTION

Objectives: As a result of this lesson, students should be able to:

(1) identify and discuss various kinds of noise pollution;
(2) identify ways to prevent noise pollution; and

(3) identify ways they can protect their own person (self) from noise pollution and cooperate with others to protect them also.

Methods and Materials:

1. Ask students to give examples of noise polluters. (Examples may include traffic, radio, television, record players, collections and deliveries, whistles and bells, construction, and loud talking and yelling.)
2. After identifying these noise polluters, try to arrive at consensus in placing them in rank order from worst to least bad.
3. Try to get a record or cassette recording of traffic noise, see if children can identify the sound, and then discuss ways in which traffic is a noise polluter in our world. (Examples may include loud mufflers, horn blowing, screeching tires, and cars and trucks with parts hanging on the ground.)
4. Have a similar discussion about each of the other noise polluters.
5. Discuss life in the country and what noise polluters exist there. (Examples are tractors, trucks, and some animals.)
6. Compare and contrast noise polluters in the city with those in the country. Ask, "Would it be possible to switch city noise polluters to the country and vice versa?"
7. Make a chart list on "How we can survive living around noise polluters."
8. As a class, write letters to environmental agencies and other groups to get more information on fighting noise pollution.
9. Make paper bag puppets with each puppet depicting noise polluting activities, such as a car's driver blowing the horn. Urge children to try to draw faces that demonstrate the emotions of the person who is doing the polluting. Have each child demonstrate the noise polluter with his or her puppet and have the class try to guess who the polluter is.

Evaluation: Observe student input during the discussion and puppet presentation.

A second lesson on noise pollution contrasts pleasing sounds with noise polluters.

LESSON 67   TREATING THE PROBLEM OF NOISE POLLUTION

Objectives: As a result of this lesson, students should be able to:

(1) identify both pleasing and disturbing sounds;

(2) demonstrate their understanding of the interdependence of noise and action or production;

(3) define noises which are necessary and those which are unnecessary to our survival; and

(4) identify noises in the environment which are considered pollutants.

Methods and Materials:

1. Have a tape recording with pleasing sounds and irritating sounds. Have each student list them, for example:

Pleasing	*Irritating*
birds singing	bells ringing
soft music	hard rock music
running water	sirens
people clapping	loud motors
trains	airplanes

1. Be sure that students understand that what one person considers to be disturbing another person might like, etc. Ask students to visualize the action they associate with the sound. (You may wish to read each sound's name and have children close their eyes to visualize the action after which they can tell each other what they visualized.)

3. Ask students what noise polluters really aren't necessary for us in our society. What could we live without? (This would be a chance to debate the SST airplanes.)

4. Ask for examples of noise polluters in the community surrounding the school. Which of the noises aren't necessary for quality living? What would be sacrificed, (for example, jobs) if the source of the sound were shut down?

5. Ask students to discuss whether or not there is a difference between noise and sound. You may wish to stretch a rubber band between two nails on a wood board. After vibrating the rubber band with your finger, ask the children if you made a noise or a sound.

6. Have students write a letter to authorities in government to get more information on noise pollution.

Evaluation: Observe student responses. Bring in records or tapes with different sounds not already discussed in class and see if students use their new understanding in discussing the sounds.

The third lesson plan on noise pollution focuses on silence as an important part of quality living.

LESSON 68   SILENCE IS GOLDEN

Objectives: As a result of this lesson, students should be able to:

(1) identify and discuss the role that silence can play in the communication process;

(2) constructively use or take advantage of quietness in the classroom setting;

(3) demonstrate an interest and some ability in communicating through the use of sign language (nonverbal language); and

(4) define the concept "language."

Methods and Materials:

1. Have signs placed around the room, such as QUIET ZONE, KEEP QUIET, SILENCE, LISTEN.

2. In order to get the children's attention and motivate them, blow a whistle or bang on a drum. Ask, "Was that a noise you heard?" "Did it hurt your ears?"

3. Give the children a few quiet minutes to sit and observe sounds and noises around them (outside and inside).

    a. List the sounds they hear on the board. Have each child classify the sounds as either *disturbing* or *enjoyable* and add other classifications if they wish.

    b. Ask, "Are any of the sounds that we heard unnecessary? Why do you think so?"

    c. Are there times when you don't like to hear any noise? When and why?

    d. Can we do without any noise at all? How would we communicate with each other? How do deaf people communicate with each other? (Sign language and lip reading will probably be mentioned. Give a brief demonstration of how sign language is used by deaf people.)

    e. Ask, "How can we use quietness in the classroom?" Have a poster for the bulletin board with their responses for quick reference in the future.

4. Children may wish to generate some guidelines or rules for quietness based on their earlier responses.

Evaluation: Observe children's understanding of the importance of silence and quiet moments, their interest in sign language and their attempts to make such signs, and their respect for "quiet rules" they decided upon for the classroom.

SUGGESTED ACTIVITIES

1. Build and distribute a list of suggestions for keeping cars from polluting the air. For example, include recommendations for when one should change oil and have engine tune-ups. Also suggest car pools.
2. Build and distribute a list of suggestions for the use of pesticides and fertilizers and the like for lawn care.
3. Make posters on the wise use of compost piles.
4. Work with the city in order to clean creek and/or river beds.
5. Build and place litter boxes around the school.
6. Build and distribute a list of suggestions for the use of household garbage in gardens, etc.
7. Inform the children that they can write the governor of their state in order to give advice as to a slogan or phrase that will be written on future license plates. A maximum of two words can be used. The theme of the slogan must be ecology. Send the letter to the governor and publish the letter and the governor's reply in the local newspaper(s).
8. Talk to several businessmen and businesswomen in the community in order to get their permission to place ecology posters in their stores. Have children place these posters and then interview businesspeople as to how the posters were received by customers.
9. Ask students to write a letter to the editor of the local newspaper in order to express two or three main ideas they have learned in their study of the environment. If the letter is published, place it in a prominent place on the bulletin board of the classroom and school.
10. Give each student a large paper shopping bag and have him or her write ECOLOGY BAG across the top of the bag. (The bag may be folded at the top or cut with pinking shears.) Then take the children on a walk through the school and on the grounds outside the school picking up any litter in the process. When the children return to the room have each child list on the front of the bag the litter he or she picked up. Discuss how the litter probably got there and how the students might prevent such littering in the future. The same activity might take place in the area surrounding the

homes of each student, with the discussion taking place at school the next day.

11. Take the children to a beach if one is nearby and have the children help collect discarded cans and the like after which you can have a good discussion about how to prevent such littering.

12. Meet with a conservation officer and have him or her explain ways in which our environment can be managed better. Have the conservation officer explain in the process what occupations are open in the area of environmental management.

13. Have the children visit an organic garden and have the gardener explain what is being done and why.

Population Control

Environmental management, strategies for fighting pollution, and population control all suggest that there is a need for achieving a balance in our lives, a balance that is a response to past mistakes. This section of the chapter relates to population control. The first lesson plan was constructed in order to give students a feel for crowded conditions due to the population explosion.

LESSON 69   THE POPULATION EXPLOSION

Objectives: As a result of this lesson, students should be able to:

(1) identify some of the difficulties associated with the population explosion, such as frustration, hostility among residents often resulting in physical violence, self-consciousness, and a feeling of despair; and

(2) suggest ways for solving or reconciling this difficult matter.

Methods and Materials:

1. Throughout this lesson, conduct your regular class in a normal way while following instructions that now follow.

2. Mark off an area in the rear of the room with enough space for four chairs jammed together.

3. Explain to the students that you will choose people to sit or stand in a limited space and you want the participants to keep a diary in which

they write their feelings about their experiences in this area during the next few days.

4. On the first day, choose two students to sit in the space.
5. Add one student the second day and one the third.
6. On the fourth day, add two more students so that students will have to remove the four desks and stand up.
7. On the fifth day have the participants read their diaries and write common feelings on the board.
8. Bring in pictures of people in the United States and other countries who live in crowded areas and ask students to write a brief essay on what it must feel like to live there. If students live in crowded conditions ask them to write an essay on what it must be like to live in a desolate rural area.
9. Have students inquire into other sources to find more information on the population explosion. Discuss possible solutions to the problem or dilemma.

Evaluation: Observe students' verbal responses and their essays.

A second grade teacher describes what happened when she used the lesson plan on the population explosion:

I asked the children, "How did it feel to be in such a tight area where you couldn't leave?" "It was hot and squishy!" one student remarked. Another added, "No one had any respect for anyone and they were pushy and noisy and I didn't like to stand." I asked, "How did you like having people coming into your circle?" A student said, "I didn't like it 'cause I had to give up my seat and stand." The last student asked to join the circle said, "I felt bad 'cause there wasn't any room for me and I had to force myself in." I then showed the children pictures of children and their parents and other adults living in crowded conditions in the city. One student said, "Why don't they leave?" Another responded, "They don't have the money and they do enjoy being with people they know will help them all they can." A girl asked, "How do they undress with all those people around?" Everyone giggled, some covered their faces, and others blushed. I responded, "It's embarrassing, but that's the way some people live in the city and in the country too even though they don't want to." I then drew a picture on the board to show that each child in the classroom could experience the population explosion in some way. But they were not able to fully comprehend this matter.

An early elementary school teacher revised the previous lesson plan somewhat as follows:

FIRST DAY: The class is divided into pairs of students with each pair given a territory, such as a small wooden territory.

Each pair will be given food to survive on (two cookies and two cartons of milk) during the 45-minute period each day when the game is played. Each pair will be given supplies to do some type of work with (1 pair of scissors, 1 bottle of glue, 1 box of crayons, 2 pencils, 14 sheets of construction paper). Work will consist of simple tasks such as cutting, pasting, coloring, etc.

Each pair will be given one trash can, but it can't be emptied until the last day of the game.

SECOND DAY: Use the same number of supplies, the same amount of food, the same territory, and the one trash can, but on this day have four students instead of two in the territory.

THIRD DAY: Use the same amount of everything used as on the first and second day, but on the final day have six students in the same territory. Ask students to keep a diary in which they record feelings each day. After three days, collect the diaries and read them carefully. Read excerpts from the diaries to the whole class with the writer's permission. After doing this for three days, have students inquire into overcrowding and overpopulation on their own and report back to the class.

LESSON 70   DENSITY AND CROWDING

Objectives: As a result of this lesson, students should be able to:

(1) discuss and evaluate the myth of unlimited resources;

(2) differentiate between "density of population" and feeling "crowded," namely that density is the actual number of people in a space and crowding is the feeling a person has when he or she perceives too many people in a space; and

(3) discuss and evaluate the myth that densely populated cities necessarily have high crime rates.

Methods and Materials:

1. Place two student volunteers in a small space in the rear of the room for a specified period of time while regular instruction occurs and give each student a cookie to eat and a chair to sit on.

2. Continue this procedure for the next few days by moving two more students in the space for a limited period of time but still issue only two cookies and two chairs.

3. When you feel this exercise has gone for a long enough time, ask the students what they learned. In particular, identify resources available to them (food, chairs, space, etc.) and ask if they believe that resources are unlimited or limited. Discuss this matter by having students cite other examples from their experiences.

4. Introduce the term "density of population" and ask students what it means. Refer to the previous exercise to demonstrate how density increased in the area in the back of the room. Ask students how density of population is determined, namely by counting the number of people in a given area.

5. Introduce the term "crowding." Ask students to list some of the characteristics of feeling crowded, such that as people bump into each other, there is little privacy, there seems to be less good air to breathe, etc.

6. Have each student choose a partner and sit back to back throughout the room. Ask students if this makes them feel crowded or not.

7. Have students sit in fairly rigid rows with little room between rows. Ask students if this makes them feel crowded or not. Ask students if their position in the room influenced their answer. For example, do you feel more crowded when most people are in front of you or behind you?

8. Discuss whether or not some people feel more crowded in some situations than others do. Why? Do large people tend to feel more crowded than small people? Do men tend to feel more crowded than women? If so, why? Do ethnic groups who have lived together for generations feel less crowded than the farmer? Why or why not?

9. Ask students to relate their views on the following generalization: Crowded cities have high crime rates because of their great population density. Ask students to try to give facts and figures to support their views after visiting the library or using other sources of information. For example, how does one explain the fact that Hong Kong has one of the lowest crime rates although its density of population is very high?

Evaluation: Observe student responses. Bring in pictures of densely populated areas and areas that are not densely populated and have students try to guess where such areas are in the world. Discuss.

LESSON 71   POPULATION CHANGES

Objectives: As a result of this lesson, students should be able to:

(1) demonstrate their awareness of the fact that populations change because of *natural increase* (births) and *migration* (movement of people from one area to another);

(2) demonstrate their awareness of the fact that technological advances in medicine have increased population by keeping fewer children from dying during birth and prolonging life thereafter; and

(3) demonstrate their awareness of the fact that technological advances in transportation have increased the mobility of people so that some areas are densely populated.

Methods and Materials:

1. Ask students for the reasons for population change: "Why does population increase and decrease?" If students have not already done so, introduce the concepts *natural increase* (births) and *migration* (movement of people from one area to another). Ask students for examples within their own experience.

2. Ask some students to investigate population changes in their own community. Have the entire class generate the kinds of questions that will aid the investigators in their inquiry: for example, who has records that we need to see and what are the particular questions we will need to ask those who hold the records?

3. Inform the students that the population of the world doubled from 1650 to 1850 and tripled from 1850 to 1950. Ask the students for reasons for this population increase. After listing reasons see which ones can be attributed to technological advances in medicine.

4. Discuss how technological advances in medicine have influenced births and the life span of people. Give examples within your own experience as a teacher and have your students do likewise. You may wish to draw upon your family tree to do so and your students may do likewise.

5. Discuss how technological advances, particularly in the field of transportation, have influenced the movement of people. Ask for experiences they have had in answering this question. For example, have there been many "For Sale" signs in their neighborhood? How about other neighborhoods in the community? Do people who work for large corporations in the community expect to live in the community for the rest of their working lives? Who pays moving expenses for corporation workers and why?

6. Ask, "How do these technological advances influence other parts of the lives of people—those who move a great deal and those who stay in the community for a lifetime?" Introduce the concepts "stability," "restlessness," "roots," and the like.

Evaluation: Identify the most densely populated states in the United States, such as New Jersey, Rhode Island, Massachusetts, Connecticut, Maryland, New York, and Delaware, and color them on a large map. Ask students if they know why these states are densely populated. Also identify California and some of the "Sun Belt" states and ask why their populations are increasing. Discuss the influence of technological changes, such as the mass production of the automobile, the availability of credit and the use of computers by lending institutions, and the building of factories, and ask what the reasons for such influence are.

The Child's World

Along with the problems of human population, there is an increasing concern for the control of our animal population. The next two lessons examine the topics of animal population control and the related topic of responsibility for a pet.

LESSON 72   CONTROLS FOR OUR PET POPULATION

Objectives: As a result of this lesson, students should be able to:

(1) discuss the dilemma of wanting their animals to have cute little offspring versus the need for animal population control; and

(2) make a decision (commitment) as to what they would do in personally facing this dilemma.

Methods and Materials:

1. Read the following case study to the children:
Carol, a second grader, loves animals. On her birthday her parents give her a beautiful little female dog. The dog is a mixed breed but Carol thinks of it as a collie. Carol calls her dog "Muffin." Carol's parents want

to take the dog to a veterinarian to have it spayed so that it won't have puppies. Carol asks her parents why they want Muffin spayed and they say: "There are already enough dogs in the world. We don't know that a litter of puppies would have good owners, and when people don't care for their dogs the dogs run wild. Wild dogs often run in packs and harm people and die without food or are killed by cars and trucks. There are simply too many dogs for the number of people who want them."

2. Discuss the dilemma of animal population control versus one's desire to have cute little offspring. Go to the board and list reasons for each position under the two headings.

3. Have a guest from the Humane Society and another guest (probably at another time) who is involved in breeding dogs. Have students decide some of the questions they wish to ask before the guests arrive.

Evaluation: Tape record the guests with their permission and discuss the tapes with the children. Have the students prepare a program on this subject for a meeting with parents such as the P.T.A.

LESSON 73   CARING FOR A PET

Objectives: As a result of this lesson, students should be able to:

(1) recognize the importance of assuming responsibility for the care of a pet;

(2) recognize that those who don't assume such responsibility shouldn't have a pet; and

(3) identify what must be done to care for a pet.

Methods and Materials:

1. Read the following story to the children:
   Mrs. Jones, a neighbor, gave Don and Karen a puppy. The children were so excited for they always wanted one but they didn't know if they should accept the puppy without asking their parents. (Should they ask their parents or just take the puppy home?) Their mother stressed the fact that pets are living things which have needs just as humans do. They also explained that caring for their pet would be completely their own responsibility. (What are some of the things the children will need to do to care for the pet?)

The children decided to work out their own schedule and arrangements to care for the pet. They decided to use a rotating system, each taking a week. This system worked well until spring when the children got involved in spring activities: both Don and Karen joined baseball teams. (Who will take care of their pet while they're at practice? Should they ask their parents to help? What would you do?)

Evaluation: Observe student responses. Have the children draw a picture of a pet they would like to own and tell or write what would have to be done to care for the pet.

Back to Nature

Children are fascinated with a variety of activities that may be categorized as back to nature activities. Camping, fishing, and hiking serve as examples. These activities give children the opportunity to integrate learnings discussed thus far in this chapter. The following lesson plan introduces the idea of returning to nature.

LESSON 74   CAMPING OUT

Objectives: As a result of this lesson, students should be able to:

(1) identify and describe the kind of equipment they need for camping out; and
(2) describe how to use the equipment in a variety of situations.

Methods and Materials:

1. Open the discussion by asking, "When you go camping, what equipment do you need?" List their responses on the board. Then ask, "Are there some items that we really don't need?"
2. Read the following to the students or have one or more students read the story to the class:
   Danny and John decided they wanted to go camping. They have never been camping before so they aren't sure what kind of equipment they will need. They especially wonder what food to take. (Ask the students if

they have any suggestions. Discuss various methods for preserving food for camping trips and the advantages and disadvantages of such methods of preservation.)

If Danny and John take a whole lot of extra things with them they won't be able to carry everything in their backpacks. Is there anything they could possibly use in place of some of the larger and heavier items available?

Danny and John want to do some hiking on their camping trip but they are somewhat afraid of getting lost. Are there some ways they might keep from getting lost?

3. Bring in a good deal of camping equipment and see if the children can guess what particular items are and how they are used. Also bring in maps of good camping areas, hiking trails, camping equipment books, and books on survival techniques in the wilderness.

4. If at all possible involve parents and others in order to provide the children with the opportunity for an overnight camping trip. This will help them try out what they've learned.

5. If an overnight trip is too difficult to do, see if the class can at least do some hiking.

Evaluation: Observe student responses. Have them interview an experienced camper and see what questions they ask.

Another teacher built the following lesson plan for her children.

LESSON 75   PREPARING TO CAMP OUT

Objectives: As a result of this lesson, students should be able to:

(1) make decisions as to how to plan a camping trip;
(2) consider environmental issues that face any camper; and
(3) communicate their views regarding these subjects to other students and the teacher.

Methods and Materials:

1. Read the following story and pause where appropriate to ask questions and involve students in discussion:

Lynn is a nine year old who enjoys the out-of-doors very much. She plans to visit her grandparents this coming weekend and invites her best friend Jill, who is also nine, to join her.

The very first night of their visit the girls plan to camp out in a wooded area of the farm. (Should the girls ask Lynn's grandfather or grandmother to help them find a good camping spot? What should the girls carry to the spot? How should they pack their supplies?)

The girls find a spot on a hillside. (Should they clear the area before setting up their camp?)

After setting up the camp, the girls decide to explore. While exploring, they get two candy bars from their pack and eat them. (What should they do with the wrappers?)

The girls gather kindling for a fire and return to camp. (What precautions should they take in building their fire? Put rocks in a circle to enclose the fire? Have a bucket of water nearby to put out sparks? Have some gas or kerosene nearby in case the fire gets low?)

The girls cook the food that Lynn's grandmother helped them prepare and then they eat. Then they decide to go to bed. (Should they put out the fire first or should they let it burn out, which will also keep any animals away from the campsite?)

They decide to leave the fire burning and awake later in the night to find smoke all around them. (Discuss how dangerous smoke can be. Should Lynn and her friend run for help or should they run and get in the nearby stream or is there some other better way to handle this situation?)

Lynn's grandfather and another nearby farmer see the smoke and put out the flames. Many trees have been destroyed. (What should Lynn's grandfather do about the trees? Plant new ones? Also plant grasses on the hills? Leave the hillside bare so no other trees will catch fire in the future?)

Evaluation: Observe student responses. Ask students to bring any camping equipment from home and discuss how it is used on a trip.

LESSON 76   A GARDEN TOUR

Objectives: As a result of this lesson, students should be able to:

(1) identify the five senses (seeing, hearing, touching-feeling, smelling, and tasting) and experience each of these senses during a garden tour;

(2) identify tools necessary to work a garden; and

(3) prepare a strawberry shortcake, thus becoming aware of the importance of others and one's independence or self-reliance.

Methods and Materials:

1. At a garden site, have a gardener show the children the tools, machines, equipment and seeds he or she uses. Have these demonstrated where possible, such as a wheelbarrow, tiller, shovel, hoe, and various seeds.

2. Divide the class into four groups with each group having a student "guide."

3. Include the following in the tour:

    a. Pulling an onion and smelling it.

    b. Picking a garden pea and opening the pod and tasting it.

    c. Shoveling a new potato and smelling the newness of the potato and the soil surrounding it.

    d. Picking a strawberry and eating it.

    e. Hearing sounds in the garden, such as bird calls, tillers and hoes.

    f. Touching the vegetables for roughness and smoothness.

4. Pick enough strawberries for making strawberry shortcake. Have the children independently:

    a. Wash their berries.

    b. De-cap them.

    c. Cut them up.

    d. Sugar them.

    e. Put on a shortcake, top with ice cream, and EAT!

Evaluation: Gather together to discuss the five senses. What colors did we see? What did we smell? What did we feel? What did we taste? What did we hear?

LESSON 77   HARVEST

Objectives: As a result of this lesson, students should be able to:

(1) list many things that grow in a garden;

(2) distinguish between the role of the gardener and the role of nature in the growing process; and

(3) develop listening skills.

Methods and Materials:

1. Show teacher-made pictures of all items seen on the garden tour:

gardener	soil
tiller	onion
wheelbarrow	potato
hoe	strawberry
shovel	garden pea

2. Play "Harvest" in pairs by providing two children with a card to share picturing four gardening items or elements. Hold up one picture. If the pair has the picture on the card they cover it with a marker. When all four pictures are covered, the pair call "Harvest!" The teacher then checks the correct responses by calling back pictures.
3. Play a variation of "Harvest" by writing a story that includes items on the card. When an item is mentioned in the story, the children can cover it. When all of their pictures are covered, they shout "Harvest!"
4. Have each child plant a seedling and place it on the window sill. When the time is right, have the children transplant the seedlings on the school grounds.

Evaluation: Have the children work together in order to create a large collage to be hung on the wall. Say that the collage should tell what the children have learned from the lesson.

LESSON 78   HOW DOES YOUR GARDEN GROW?

Objectives: As a result of this lesson, students should be able to:

(1) express in words where specific vegetables and strawberries grow;
(2) demonstrate on a flannelboard what elements are necessary to make a garden grow; and
(3) feel a kind of independence in planting a seed while still recognizing a kind of dependence on nature and its forces.

Methods and Materials:

1. Sit in front of the children with a grocery bag containing garden vege-

tables and fruit; hold each item in the air and have children identify each one by name:

radish	lettuce
onion	strawberry
potato	garden pea

2. Ask the students where these items grow? How do they grow? Do they grow above or below ground?
3. Provide a flannelboard to illustrate how a garden grows. Include: sun, rain, soil, seeds to plants.
4. Provide each child with a base of a milk carton, potting soil, and seeds for planting.
5. Have each child draw a picture of the kind of vegetable or flower he or she is growing and fasten the picture to the container.
6. Have the children water their seeds and place them in a sunny area. Care for the seedlings until they are plants and then transplant to a special place.

Evaluation: To the tune of "Mulberry Bush," have the children sing and pantomime the planting process. Ask children to classify vegetables according to color, bulbs, leaves, berries, and inside or outside seeds.

LESSON 79   ORGANIC GARDENING

Objectives: As a result of this lesson, students should be able to:

(1) discuss and evaluate the generalization that natural means for combating plant disease and encouraging plant growth are both possible and preferable to man-made means for such purposes in many instances;
(2) identify and discuss pros and cons of technological means for improving agriculture; and
(3) participate in organic gardening experiences.

Methods and Materials:

1. Discuss with students many and diverse technological "advances" in agriculture, such as new kinds of machinery and chemicals. Bring to class pictures of many of these changes. (Advertisers will provide you with such materials free of charge.) Write pros on one side of the

blackboard and cons on the other and list pros and cons in each column for particular "advances."

2. Discuss the differences between organic fertilizers or conditioners, organic disease fighters, and man-made fertilizers or conditioners and disease fighters. Show pictures of each. (You may want to assign this task to children for the next day.)

3. Read the following story to the children:

Mr. Andrews decided to plant a garden this year. He wants to plant corn, tomatoes, cucumbers, squash, lettuce, onions, and radishes. Like all gardeners, he hopes to have a plentiful garden with a good crop yield. Mrs. Andrews suggested the use of organic methods primarily for safety purposes for she worries about the effects of chemicals. Mr. Andrews wants to use commercial chemicals because it is less work.

   a. List the reasons why each person, Mr. Andrews and Mrs. Andrews, would want to have his or her way in this conflict. Then state your position in this regard.

   Organic Methods   Chemical Methods

   b. Have a class debate on this matter with each side researching its case and presenting pictures and other audio-visual aids to illustrate arguments.

4. See if you and your class can use a piece of land somewhere near the school and use organic methods in half of your garden and chemical methods in the other half of the garden. Teach students to keep a running record of the two gardens in a small notebook.

Evaluation: Observe student responses. Invite an advocate of organic gardening and an advocate of the use of chemicals for gardening into your class and see if students' questions and discussion demonstrate a grasp of key concepts and generalizations.

LESSON 80   BUILDING A NATURE TRAIL

Objectives: As a result of this lesson, students should be able to:

(1) actively participate in building a nature trail by surveying a natural area of land, drawing a map of where the trail should be, constructing directional and informational signs to be placed on the trail, and designing a mimeograph brochure concerning use of the trail.

Methods and Materials:

1. Initiate contact with a citizen in the community, preferably near the school, who is interested in preserving the wilderness as it is. Ask this person if you and your students can build a nature trail to be used primarily by the school children in the school where you teach.

2. Bring to class a guest who is knowledgeable about surveying land. This person should have background in surveying and nature study if possible. Take students and the surveyor to the site after planning for the survey itself.

   a. Have each student draw a map of the land with the nature trail on the map. Discuss students maps and decide as a class where the nature trail should be on the land.

3. Involve the class in the actual building of the trail using any advisors you can acquire from the community.

4. Gather appropriate lumber, nails, etc., and construct directional and informational signs to be placed on the trail.

5. Take other classes on the trail and make further refinements of the trail based on students' responses.

6. Work and play with the class to design and produce a brochure describing the trail. Make the brochure as graphic as possible with a map, etc.

7. Distribute the brochure to the entire student body and systematically ask for responses to the brochure. Refine the brochure for a second printing if such revisions are required.

Evaluation: Observe student responses. Devise a check list of behaviors to look for as students participate in this project. Invite an "expert" from out-of-town to evaluate the nature trail. His or her expertise should be based on involvement in nature trail construction in his or her own community.

LESSON 81   BACK-TO-NATURE CAREERS

Objectives: As a result of this lesson, students should be able to:

   (1) define and discuss horticulture and careers related to it; and

   (2) demonstrate application of their knowledge by planting their own garden on school grounds.

Methods and Materials:

1. Prepare a bulletin board as follows: Cut the shape of a flower pot from

poster board and add flowers and foliage from scraps of materials. On the leaves place pictures of different occupations: florist, garden shop owner, conservationist, farmer, and gardener. Print the title of the bulletin board HORTICULTURE on the flower pot.

2. Discuss the meaning of horticulture and how each job relates to the term.

3. Invite persons from horticultural occupations to class to discuss their work.

4. Prepare a small vegetable garden as a class and discuss the process of creating such a garden as you go along. Have the garden on school grounds or nearby if possible.

Evaluation: Make daily observations of vegetable growth and develop a systematic method for recording such growth. Occasionally pick up student responses and react to them in their record books (logs).

Conclusion

The future of our planet will depend in large measure on how we teach environmental education to children in our elementary schools. When children's initial curiosity about the environment is wedded with firm understandings about a healthy environment, the student is well on the way to effective citizenship. In this part we have focused on this challenge, and in the process tried to help the child and teacher feel better about himself or herself and about relationships with others.

Epilogue

At the beginning of this book you were asked to help create a map for your exploration through the various activities I included. By now you have experienced the many emotions associated with exploration: exhilaration, joy, fear, and even perhaps some anger. But my guess is that you discovered that the journey was worth it, for you were actively involved in learning along with your children in a variety of learning settings. This is another way of saying that you answered the questions WHO'S TEACHING—WHO'S LEARNING? by saying "The students *and* I, for we were all actively involved in creating our own settings." Your answer reflects the good feeling that comes with meeting new challenges, challenges that give vitality to our lives in general and teaching in particular. My message to you is BON VOYAGE as we continue our journey as teachers and learners.

NOTES

1. Robert Roth's writing was very helpful to the author in this section of the chapter. See "Fundamental Concepts for Environmental Management Education," *Environmental Education*, 1, no. 3 (Spring 1970), pp. 69—73.

2. Pat Mattern was most helpful in revising the lesson plan story titled "L.J. Builds a Treehouse."